Black Faculty in the Academy

D1564166

Through candid discussions and personal counter-narrative stories, *Black Faculty in the Academy* explores the experiences and challenges faced by faculty of color in academe. Black faculty in predominantly White college and university settings must negotiate multiple and competing identities while struggling with issues of marginality, otherness, and invisible... develop a professional ide... time remaining true to cultu... authors situate race-related... to deconstruct and challeng... ey also provide key recomm... their continued professional... how faculty can successfully... ding tenure and promotion, p... ith institutional climate issue... eking to create an environm... s among Black faculty.

Fred A. Bon... n the Graduate School of E... SA.

aretha faye ... ng in Counselor Education at...

Frank Tuitt ... te Provost for Inclusive Ex...

Petra A. Rol... urce Education and Workfor...

Rosa M. Ba... Chair in Education in the C... versity of New Jersey, USA.

PRINTED IN U.S.A.

DATE DUE

Robin L. Hughes is Associate Professor in the Department of Educational Leadership and Policy Studies, Higher Education Student Affairs at Indiana University Indianapolis, USA.

Black Faculty in the Academy

Narratives for Negotiating Identity and Achieving Career Success

**Edited by
Fred A. Bonner II,
aretha faye marbley,
Frank Tuitt,
Petra A. Robinson,
Rosa M. Banda, and
Robin L. Hughes**

Routledge
Taylor & Francis Group

NEW YORK AND LONDON

First published 2015
by Routledge
711 Third Avenue, New York, NY 10017

and by Routledge
2 Park Square, Milton Park, Abingdon, Oxon, OX14 4RN

Routledge is an imprint of the Taylor & Francis Group, an informa business

© 2015 Taylor & Francis

Library of Congress Cataloging-in-Publication Data
Black faculty in the academy : narratives for negotiating identity and
    achieving career success / [edited] by Fred A. Bonner II, Aretha Faye
    Marbley, Frank Tuitt, Petra A. Robinson, Rosa M. Banda, and Robin L.
    Hughes.
        pages cm
    Includes bibliographical references and index.
    1. African American college teachers—Social conditions.   2. African
American college teachers—Job satisfaction.   3. Faculty integration—
United States.   4. Discrimination in higher education—United States.
I. Bonner, Fred A.
    LC2781.5.B528   2014
    378.1′982996073—dc23
    2014026372

ISBN: 978-0-415-72754-9 (hbk)
ISBN: 978-0-415-72755-6 (pbk)
ISBN: 978-1-315-85216-4 (ebk)

Typeset in Perpetua and Bell Gothic
by Apex CoVantage, LLC

Printed and bound in the United States of America by Publishers Graphics,
LLC on sustainably sourced paper.

CONTENTS

7 Using Endarkened and Critical Race Feminist Perspectives to Question and Analyze Knowledge Production Narratives 67
Natasha N. Croom and Lori D. Patton

8 Navigating Race-Gendered Microaggressions: The Experiences of a Tenure-Track Black Female Scholar 79
Dorinda J. Carter Andrews

9 Black Queer (Re)presentation in (White) Academe: I am the Hell and the High Water 89
Dafina-Lazarus Stewart

PART III
Black Faculty: Finding Strength through Critical Mentoring Relationships 103

10 Self-Reflection as a Critical Tool in the Life of an Early Career African American Male Scholar 105
Alonzo M. Flowers III

11 Engaging Mentoring Relationships in Academia: Hard Lessons Learned 115
Buffy Smith

12 The Critical Need for Faculty Mentoring: Say Brother, Can You Spare the Time? 123
Fred A. Bonner II

13 Establishing Critical Relationships with Students: That's Not What White Professor "X" Told Us 137
Saundra M. Tomlinson-Clarke

Notes on Contributors 147
Index 155

Preface

Sojourner Truth's moving speech "Ain't I a Woman," delivered before the assembled masses at the 1851 Women's Rights Convention held in Akron, Ohio, served as a cynosure for generations of women—particularly African American women and other women of color—who sought to find some sense of agency in a racist and sexist America. Just as Sojourner's speech captured the plight of women and African Americans in their pursuit of freedom and liberation from a hostile society, so too do her words frame the extant experiences of faculty of color who teach in predominantly White college and university settings.

According to Stanley (2006), a host of phrases and terms have been identified to describe the experiences of faculty of color in these institutional settings; namely, multiple marginality; multiple oppressions; otherness; living in two worlds; the academy's new cast; silenced voices; ivy halls and glass walls; individual survivors or institutional transformers; from border to center; visible and invisible barriers; the color of teaching; and navigating between two worlds. Each phrase and term in some capacity contributes to how faculty of color not only frame their experiences in the academy but also how they go about establishing some sense of identity.

For Black faculty, "fitting in" means developing a professional identity that is congruent with the mores, values, and traditions of the academy, one that is oftentimes at odds with the cultural, social, and personal identities that these faculty members bring to the academy (Bonner, 2004; Fries-Britt & Kelly, 2005; Heggens, 2004; Patitu & Hinton, 2003; Stanley, 2006). According to Turner and Myers (2000), recalcitrance by the academy to modify traditional practices and policies, accentuated by both covert and overt acts found detrimental to the success of Blacks and other groups of color at predominantly White colleges and universities, continues to reify the "chilly climate" faculty of color often identify in these contexts.

Chapters in this book are supported by critical race theory (CRT) (Ladson-Billings, 1999; Solórzano, Ceja, & Yoso, 2000; Tate, 1997) as the theoretical foundation as well as operationalized through the use of Scholarly Personal Narrative (SPN) as the key methodological approach. Initiated and advocated by Robert Nash, SPN honors and values personal stories. SPN provides an opportunity to go beyond the traditional boundaries of qualitative research as it places the "self of the scholar front and center" (Nash, 2004, p. 18). As an alternative form of intellectual inquiry, SPN is particularly relevant for these chapters as it encourages and even demands writing in the first-person voice. In academia, there is typically little (if any) opportunity to write using such an "authentic and person-centered" tradition; such has been particularly true for "people of color who have had to suppress their strong distinct voices, along with their anger, for years in the academy" (Nash, 2004, p. 2). Thus using SPN as a methodological approach underscores the relevance and appropriateness of the methodology for this volume.

In the tradition of CRT, each chapter author creates personal counternarratives that depict creative interpretations of their lived experiences as Black faculty negotiating multiple and competing identities within predominantly White institutions—told through the use of SPN. Ultimately, each chapter author will situate race-related encounters at the center of their lived experience in an effort to deconstruct and challenge commonly held assumptions about life in academe for Black faculty.

CRITICAL RACE THEORY

In *Black Faculty in the Academy: Narratives for Negotiating Identity and Achieving Career Success*, chapter authors use critical race theory (CRT) (Ladson-Billings, 1999; Solórzano, Ceja, & Yosso, 2000; Tate, 1997) as a theoretical and methodological foundation for exploring their narratives experiences of teaching in PWIs. CRT is a useful framework for the examination of the impact of race because it accounts for the role of racism in U.S. education and works toward the elimination of racism as a part of a larger goal of eliminating all forms of subordination in education (Yosso, 2002).

The exact inception of CRT is unknown, although numerous scholars (Crenshaw, Gotanda, Peller, & Thomas, 1995; Delgado & Stefancic, 2001; Tate, 1997) trace the foundational roots of CRT to the 1970s in the midst of the post-Civil Rights era. However, in 1994, CRT was introduced into the field of education by Gloria Ladson-Billings and William Tate (Ladson-Billings, 2005). Despite its relatively short existence, numerous education scholars have embraced CRT including Solorzano and Yosso (2001), Yosso (2002), Ladson-Billings (2005), and Tate (1997). Since the incorporation of CRT into education, scholars have utilized this theoretical and methodological framework to critically analyze both education research and practice. Specifically, educational scholars have relied upon CRT to address school discipline and hierarchy, affirmative action, curriculum development, the presentation of history, standardized testing, meritocracy, and the lived educational experiences of people of color (Crenshaw, Gotanda, Peller, & Thomas, 1995; Delgado & Stefancic, 2001; Solorzano & Yosso, 2001; Yosso, 2002). It is this last point, "the lived experiences of Black faculty," that will serve to ground this volume. Specifically, CRT will allow each of the chapter authors to situate race related encounters at the center of their collective lived experiences in an effort to deconstruct and challenge commonly held assumptions about life in academe for faculty of color.

CRITICAL RACE THEORY AND COUNTER-NARRATIVES

In the tradition of CRT, each chapter author creates personal counter-narratives that depict creative interpretations of their lived experiences as Black faculty at predominantly White institutions. According to Ladson Billings (1999), personal narratives and stories are important in truly understanding lived experiences and how those experiences may represent confirmation or counter-knowledge of the way society works. She contends that stories are used to analyze the myths, pre-suppositions, and received wisdoms that make up the common culture about race. To that end, in this presentation our collective counter-narratives will explore and utilize shared and individual experiences of race, gender, imagination, status, language, and sexuality in education (Solorzano, 1997; Yosso, 2002). Our hope is that the analysis of the chapter author's collective experiences in academe will contribute to the development of a critical literacy whereas emerging scholars of color we are able to use the language and our voices contained in our counter-narratives to examine the impact of racial identities on the experiences of Black faculty in PWIs (Sleeter & Delgado Bernal, 2003).

REFERENCES

Bonner, F. A. (2004). Black professors: On the track but out of the loop. *Chronicle of Higher Education, 50*(40), B11–B11.

Crenshaw, K., Gotanda, N., Peller, G., & Thomas, K. (2000). *Critical Race Theory: The key writings that formed the movement.* New York: The New York Press.

Delgado, R., & Stefancic, J. (2001). *Critical Race Theory: An introduction.* New York: New York University Press.

Fries-Britt, S. L., & Kelly-Turner, B. (2005). Retaining each other: Narratives of two African American women in the academy. *The Urban Review, 37*(3), 221–242.

Heggins, W. J. (2004). Preparing African American males for the professoriate: Issues and Challenges. *Western Journal of Black Studies, 28*(2), 354–364.

Ladson-Billings, G. (1999). Preparing teachers for diverse student populations: A critical race theory perspective. In A. Iran-Nejad & P. D. Pearson (Eds.), *Review of Research in Higher Education: Volume 24* (pp. 211–247). Washington: American Educational Research Association.

Ladson-Billings, G. (2005). The evolving role of critical race theory in educational scholarship. *Race Ethnicity and Education, 8*(1), 115–119.

Stanley, C. A. (Ed.). (2006). *Faculty of color: Teaching in predominantly white colleges and universities.* Boston, MA: Anker Publishing Company, Inc.

Nash, R. J. (2004). *Liberating scholarly writing: The power of personal narrative.* New York: Teachers College Press.

Patitu, C. L., & Hinton, K. G. (2003). The experiences of African American women faculty and administrators in higher education: Has anything changed? *New Directions for Student Services, 104*, 79–93.

Sleeter, C. E., & Delgado, Bernal, E. (2003). Critical pedagogy, critical race theory, and antiracist education. In J. A. Banks & C. A. Banks (Eds.), *Handbook of research on multicultural education* (2nd ed.). San Francisco: Jossey Bass.

Solorzano, D. G. (1997). Images and words that wound: Critical race theory, racial stereotyping, and teacher education. *Teacher Education Quarterly, 24*(3), 5–19.

Solorzano, D., Ceja, M., & Yosso, T. (2000). Critical Race Theory, racial microaggessions, and campus racial climate: The experiences of African American college students. *Journal of Negro Education, 69*(1/2), 60–73.

Solorzano, D., & Yosso, T. J. (2001). Critical race and LatCrit theory and method: Counter-storytelling. *Qualitative Studies in Education, 14*(4), 471–495.

Tate, W. F. (1997). Critical Race Theory and education: History, theory, and implications. *Review of Research, 22*, 195–247.

Turner, C. S., & Myers, S. L. (2000). *Faculty of color: Bittersweet success.* San Francisco: Jossey-Bass.

Yosso, T. J. (2002). Toward a critical race curriculum. *Equity and Excellence, 35*(2), 93–107.

Chapter 1

Introduction

Frank Tuitt and Fred A. Bonner II

The genesis for this book emerged out the growing awareness that even though some progress has been made in the academy regarding its efforts to provide a more diverse and inclusive campus setting, for some faculty of color, an unwelcoming and potentially hostile campus environment awaits those who choose to teach in predominantly White institutions (PWIs) (Stanley, 2006; Trower, 2003; Tuitt, Danowitz, & Sotello-Turner, 2007). For example, according to Stanley (2006), a host of phrases and terms have been identified to describe the experiences of faculty of color in these institutional settings; namely, *multiple marginality; multiple oppressions; otherness; living in two worlds; the academy's new cast; silenced voices; ivy halls and glass walls; individual survivors or institutional transformers; from border to center; visible and invisible barriers; the color of teaching; and navigating between two worlds.* The unfortunate reality is that many faculty of color willingly come to work with the full understanding that they are more likely to be scrutinized and held to higher standards (McGowan, 2000), marginalized and devalued (Turner & Myers, 2000), and teach in the line of fire (Tuitt, Hanna, Martinez, Salazar, & Griffin, 2009).

The conditions and experiences such as those described above counter prevailing notions of a post-racial academy (Carter-Andrews & Tuitt, 2013) and have significant implications for how faculty members of color in general and Black faculty specifically, negotiate their personal, political, and professional interactions in the academy. Accordingly, a central focus of this book is to provide deeper understanding of how Black faculty not only frame their experiences in the academy but also how they go about establishing some sense of identity. We explore the lived experiences of Black faculty recognizing that our "fitting in," which often means, for some of us, attempting to develop a professional identity that is congruent with the mores, values, and traditions of the academy, cannot be separated from the historical, contextual, and systemic oppression of Black people in this country. Thus Black professors' efforts to successfully navigate the academy are oftentimes in direct conflict with the cultural, social, and personal identities that they bring to the work environment (Bonner, 2004; Fries-Britt & Kelly-Turner, 2005; Heggins, 2004; Patitu & Hinton, 2003; Stanley, 2006).

CRITICAL RACE THEORY

In this volume many of the authors use critical race theory (CRT) (Ladson-Billings, 1999; Solórzano, Ceja, & Yosso, 2000; Tate, 1997) as a theoretical and methodological foundation for constructing and analyzing narratives of their lived experiences in the academy. According to several scholars, CRT is a useful framework for the examination of the impact of race and the role of racism in U.S. higher education (Yosso, 2002). The exact inception of CRT is unknown, although numerous scholars (Crenshaw, Gotanda, Peller, & Thomas, 1996; Delgado & Stefancic, 2001; Tate, 1997) trace the foundational roots of CRT to legal scholarship of the late 1970s post-Civil Rights era. Derrick Bell, legal scholar and professor, is considered the founder of CRT, establishing many of its initial conceptual and analytic arguments through his radicalized deconstruction and formidable legal decisions including *Brown v. Board of Education, Topeka Kansas* (Bell, 1979). However, in 1994, CRT was introduced into the field of education by Gloria Ladson-Billings and William Tate (Ladson-Billings, 2005). Since its introduction, scholars have utilized this theoretical and methodological framework to critically analyze both education research and practice. CRT is typically guided by six tenets or unifying themes (Dixson & Rousseau, 2005). These six tenets are as follows:

1. Racism is endemic to American life.
2. Dominant ideologies of race neutrality, objectivity, colorblindness, and meritocracy are viewed with skepticism.
3. Racism has contributed to all contemporary manifestations of group advantage and disadvantage.
4. The experiential knowledge of people of color must be recognized.
5. CRT is interdisciplinary.
6. Elimination of racial oppression is the focus of CRT as part of the broader goal of ending all forms of oppression.

Drawing upon these tenets, and through the construction of new tenets, educational scholars have harnessed CRT to address topics such as school discipline and hierarchy, affirmative action, curriculum development, the presentation of history, standardized testing, meritocracy, and the lived educational experiences of people of color (Crenshaw et al., 1996; Delgado & Stefancic, 2001; Solórzano & Yosso, 2001; Yosso, 2002).

2

CRITICAL RACE METHODOLOGY

The chapter authors in this volume employ a critical race methodology to explore their racialized experiences as Black faculty in the academy. Specifically they embrace Solórzano and Yosso's (2002) definition of a critical race methodology as a theoretical approach to research that (a) foregrounds race and racism in all aspects of the research process; (b) challenges the traditional research paradigms, texts, and theories used to explain the experiences of people of color; (c) offers a libertory or transformative solution to racial, gender, and class subordination; and (d) focuses on the racialized, gendered, and classed experiences of people of color. Furthermore, by employing critical race methodology to explore the experiences of Black faculty, the chapter authors view these experiences as sources of strength and (e) use the interdisciplinary knowledge base of ethnic studies, women's studies, sociology, history, humanities, and the law to better understand these collective lived experiences (Solórzano & Yosso, 2002). It is this last point, *the lived experiences of Black faculty*, that grounds this volume. Specifically, by employing a critical race methodology each of the chapter authors situate their race-related encounters at the center of their collective lived experiences in an effort to deconstruct and challenge commonly held assumptions about life in academe for Black faculty.

CRITICAL RACE THEORY AND COUNTER-NARRATIVES

In the tradition of CRT, each chapter author was invited to create personal counter-narratives that depict creative interpretations of some aspect of their lived experiences as Black faculty at predominantly White institutions. To that end, each chapter applies CRT as the theoretical foundation as well as the key operationalized methodological approach through the use of Scholarly Personal Narrative (SPN). Initiated and advocated by Robert Nash (2004), SPN honors and values personal stories. SPN provides an opportunity to go beyond the traditional boundaries of qualitative research as it places the "self of the scholar front and center" (Nash, 2004, p. 18). An alternative form of intellectual inquiry, SPN is particularly relevant for these chapters as it encourages and even demands writing in the first-person voice. In academia, there is typically little (if any) opportunity to write using such an "authentic and person-centered" tradition; such has been particularly true for "people of color who have had to suppress their strong distinct voices, along with their anger, for years in the academy" (Nash, 2004, p. 2). Thus using SPN as a methodological approach underscores the relevance and appropriateness of the methodology for this volume.

As a collection, the Scholarly Personal Narratives offer a unique and important opportunity for readers to truly understand lived experiences of Black faculty

3

and how those experiences represent confirmation or counter-knowledge of the manifestation of race and racism in the academy. Correspondingly, the SPNs in this book offer creative interpretations of the lived experiences of Black faculty as they negotiate multiple and competing identities within PWIs and at the same time allow readers to analyze and critique the myths, presuppositions, and received wisdoms that often lead some to view colleges and universities as post-racial or race neutral (Ladson-Billings, 1999).

APPLICATION OF CRITICAL RACE THEORY AND METHODOLOGY

In addition to using CRT as a methodology for constructing Scholarly Personal Narratives, each of the chapters in this book utilizes critical race theory as an analytical framework that empowers chapter authors to make meaning of their lived experiences. In their application of CRT, the authors collectively identify three core thematic trends that emerge throughout the chapters in this volume related to Black faculty:

1. navigating daily encounters with racism;
2. meaning making through interdisciplinary and intersectional approaches; and
3. finding strength through critical mentoring relationships.

While several of the chapters speak to one or more of these three areas we have grouped the chapters based on our reading of their main focus. What follows is a brief introduction to each of the three primary areas and the related chapters that contribute to a collective understanding of the lived experiences of Black faculty.

Black Faculty: Navigating Daily Encounters with Racism

Many of the chapters in this book remind us that in spite of incremental advancements for diversity on our college campuses throughout the country, racism remains a permanent vestige of American higher education. To illuminate some of the current manifestations of racism in the academy, several of the authors use CRT to contest colorblind, objective, and meritocratic discourses that promote the illusion of a level playing field (Dixson & Rousseau, 2005). Their counter-narratives offer rich testimonies revealing how Black faculty are forced to navigate the work environment carrying a racial burden which makes their experience uniquely and qualitatively different from their White counterparts (Harlow, 2003). For example, in Chapters 2, 3, 4, and 5 the authors provide insight into how the racial "threats in the air" (Steele, 1997) are more than just a figments of their imagination but real life encounters with microaggressions and

4

macro invalidations which serve as daily reminders that even though they may have the same title as their White counterparts they are still a guest in somebody else's house (Turner & Myers, 2000). Specifically, in Chapter 2, Mark Giles applies CRT to examine several layers of his life experiences related to navigating a "chilly" institutional climate while studying and working at predominately White institutions (PWIs). Similarly, in Chapter 3, Ariel William Moore adds to the discussion Black faculty daily encounters with racism by interrogating his personal experiences and struggles with historical legacies and contemporary practices of exclusion and marginality in the academy. In Chapter 4, Anton Lewis and Katherine Helm employ a CRT perspective to examine the centrality of race and racism as Black faculty connected to their experiences of "social networking within the Academy." Through their exploration readers are able to discern how Black voices are left out, misunderstood, perceived as threatening or angry, and frequently discounted or silenced. Marjorie C. Shavers, J. Yasmine Butler, and James L. Moore round out this section by investigating the dilemma Black faculty face related to hidden service expectations and cultural taxation which often results in their spending more time on activities that do not promote their professional socialization while diminishing their chances for attaining tenure and promotions. They conclude their chapter by offering research supported strategies that can balance the academic landscape for Black faculty. Overall, the chapters in this section contest contemporary forms of post-racial discourse by foregrounding the broader structural inequalities that continue to marginalize and oppress Black faculty (Ladson-Billings, 1998).

Black Faculty: Meaning Making through Multidisciplinary and Intersectional Approaches

Several of the chapters in this volume utilize an interdisciplinary and intersectional approach to make meaning of their individual and collective experiences of race, gender, class, language, and sexuality in education (Solórzano, 1997; Yosso, 2002). In this regard their stories are unapologetically race intercentric, in that their analysis centralizes race and racism with other forms of systemic oppression, recognizing the multiple layers of identity that shape their lived experiences (Yosso, 2002). For example, in Chapters 6, 7, 8, and 9, the authors provide an intersectional analysis of their lived experiences as Black women in the academy by leveraging multiple disciplinary perspectives and frameworks. Specifically, in Chapter 6, aretha marbley, Leon Rouson, Jiaqi Li, Shih-Han Huang, and Colette Taylor use critical race theory and critical feminist theories to analyze the lived experiences of Black faculty and Black women faculty recognizing that the personal is always political and as such the alienating, racist, sexist, stressful, chilly, and unwelcoming climate they encounter is not a story of individual struggle but one of group struggle resulting from methodical and systemic oppression.

Similarly, in Chapter 7 Natasha Croom and Lori Patton use an endarkened feminist epistemology to explain how they come to acquire and make meaning of knowledge and critical race feminism (CRF) as a lens of analysis to explicate the racism and sexism that invades their experiences as Black women faculty. Additionally, in Chapter 8, Dorinda Carter Andrews engages Black feminist thought (BFT) to examine two aspects of the double jeopardy that Black women professors experience in the academy: the raced-gendered challenges with legitimation as a scholar and existence as an 'insider-outsider' (Collins, 1993) in her department. Similarly, in Chapter 9, Dafina-Lazarus Stewart combines Black feminist thought and critical race theory to examine the intersection of race, sexuality, and gender identity and expression in her experiences as a faculty member. Together these chapters acknowledge the intercentricity of racialized oppression—layers of subordination based on race, gender, class, and sexuality (Solórzano & Yosso, 2002).

Black Faculty: Finding Strength through Critical Mentoring Relationships

The remaining chapters in the book provide insight into how critical mentoring relationships are as they can serve as a buffer to, and liberating or transformative solution from, the racialized isolation Black faculty experience in PWIs. For example, in Chapter 10, Alonzo Flowers showcases his thoughts and experiences in his first two years as an assistant professor that resulted from extensive critical dialogue exchanges with a colleague. Likewise, in Chapter 11, Buffy Smith explores the influence of her formal and informal mentors who were the most important colleagues in helping her understand and navigate the hidden curriculum of the university while providing support and strategies for managing the impact of institutional racism, sexism, and heterosexism. In Chapter 12, Fred Bonner's Scholarly Personal Narrative begins from a very personal space with a story that is intimately connected to his focus on his own *emic* experiences as an African American man who has not only researched the experiences of faculty of color in postsecondary contexts, but also as an intrepid traveler who has been on a 16-year voyage attempting to make his way to the higher education *promised land*. Bonner attributes his success during his trek to his mentors who served as guides that have been an ever-present force in keeping him apprised of impending dangers as well as motivated to keep moving when stalling or stopping seemed to be his only options. While Bonner, Flowers, and Smith reflect on the support and encouragement they received from faculty colleagues, in Chapter 13, Saundra Tomlinson-Clarke reflects on the rewards, challenges, and lessons learned that shaped her realities and defined what she considers to be critical in establishing relationships with students as a Black, woman, tenured faculty member at a predominantly White, research university. This collection of chapters remind us that critical mentoring relationships can provide Black faculty with a vehicle for self-preservation as well as a balm that can work to heal the wounds caused by racial oppression (Ladson-Billings, 1998).

Overall our hope, as editors, is that this book and its compilation of lived experiences contributes to the development of a critical literacy where scholars and practitioners would be able to use the voices and insights contained in the 12 counter-narratives to examine the impact of multiple identities on the experiences of Black faculty in PWIs (Sleeter & Delgado Bernal, 2003). As a collection, the chapters in this book address the long-standing dilemma of how Black faculty can develop a professional identity that leads to their success in academe, while at the same time remaining true to their cultural and personal identities. Additionally, this book provides a focused dialogue on the topic of "otherness" in an attempt to assist those in the academy who are responsible for the retention of faculty of color in understanding what it means to establish a professional identity as a member of a minority group while functioning in a majority context. By excogitating the experiences presented through formal narratives, our hope is that Black faculty will be able to identify salient themes across these personal accounts that contribute to the development of their professional identities. Additionally, the book will provide readers with key recommendations to facilitate the creation and establishment of critical departmental initiatives to aid in the development of healthy professional identities among Black faculty across academic disciplines and within faculty hierarchical structures. As you read this book we hope that you are motivated in the spirit of critical race theory to join us in this project of change where we heed the call to action to not only critique racism in the academy but to get involved in the labor for social transformation, to roll up your sleeves and work toward the elimination of racial oppression as a part of the broader goal of ending all forms of oppression.

REFERENCES

Bell, D. A. (1979). Brown v. Board of Education and the interest-convergence dilemma. *Harvard Law Review*, *93*, 518–533.

Bonner, F. A. (2004). Black professors: On the track but out of the loop. *Chronicle of Higher Education, 50*(40), B11–B11.

Carter-Andrews, D., & Tuitt, F. (2013). *Contesting the myth of a post-racial era: The continued significance of race in U.S. education*. New York, NY: Peter Lang Publishing.

Collins, P. H. (1993). *Black feminist thought: Knowledge, consciousness, and the politics of empowerment*. New York, NY: Routledge.

Crenshaw, K., Gotanda, N., Peller, G., & Thomas, K. (1996). *Critical race theory: The key writings that formed the movement*. New York, NY: New York Press.

Delgado, R., & Stefancic, J. (2001). *Critical race theory: An introduction*. New York, NY: New York University Press.

Dixson, A., & Rousseau, C. K. (2005). And we are still not saved: Critical race theory in education ten years later. *Race, Ethnicity, and Education, 8*(1), 7–27.

Fries-Britt, S. L., & Kelly-Turner, B. (2005). Retaining each other: Narratives of two African American women in the academy. *The Urban Review, 37*(3), 221–242.

Heggins, W. J. (2004). Preparing African American males for the professoriate: Issues and challenges. *Western Journal of Black Studies, 28*(2), 354–364.

Harlow, R. (2003). "Race doesn't matter, but . . .": The effect of race on professors' experiences and emotion management in the undergraduate college classroom. *Social Psychology Quarterly, 66*(4), 348–363.

Ladson-Billings, G. (1998). Just what is critical race theory and what's it doing in a nice field like education? *International Journal of Qualitative Studies in Education, 11*(1), 7–24.

Ladson-Billings, G. (1999). Preparing teachers for diverse student populations: A critical race theory perspective. In A. Iran-Nejad, & P. D. Pearson (Eds.), *Review of research in higher education: Volume 24* (pp. 211–247). Washington: American Educational Research Association.

Ladson-Billings, G. (2005). The evolving role of critical race theory in educational scholarship. *Race Ethnicity and Education, 8*(1), 115–119.

McGowan, J. (2000). Multicultural teaching: African-American faculty classroom teaching experience in predominantly White colleges and universities. *Multicultural Education, 8*(2), 19–22.

Nash, R. J. (2004). *Liberating scholarly writing: The power of personal narrative*. New York, NY: Teachers College Press.

Patitu, C. L., & Hinton, K. G. (2003). The experiences of African American women faculty and administrators in higher education: Has anything changed? *New Directions for Student Services, 104*, 79–93.

Sleeter, C. E., & Delgado Bernal, D. (2003). Critical pedagogy, critical race theory, and antiracist education. In J. A. Banks, & C. A. Banks (Eds.), *Handbook of research on multicultural education* (2nd ed., pp. 240–260). San Francisco: Jossey-Bass.

Solórzano, D. G. (1997). Images and words that wound: Critical race theory, racial stereotyping, and teacher education. *Teacher Education Quarterly, 24*(3), 5–19.

Solórzano, D., Ceja, M., & Yosso, T. (2000). Critical race theory, racial microaggressions, and campus racial climate: The experiences of African American college students. *Journal of Negro Education, 69*(1 / 2), 60–73.

Solórzano, D., & Yosso, T. (2001). Critical race and LatCrit theory and method: Counter-storytelling. *Qualitative Studies in Education, 14*(4), 471–495.

Solórzano, D., & Yosso, T. (2002). Critical race methodology: Counter-storytelling as an analytical framework for education research. *Qualitative Inquiry, 8*(1), 23–44.

Stanley, C. A. (Ed.). (2006). *Faculty of color: Teaching in predominantly White colleges and universities*. Bolton, MA: Anker Publishing Company, Inc.

Steele, C. M. (1997). A threat in the air: How stereotypes shape intellectual identity and performance. *American Psychologist, 52*(6), 613–629.

Tate, W. F. (1997). Critical race theory and education: History, theory, and implications. *Review of Research, 22*, 195–247.

Trower, C. A. (2003). Leveling the field. *Academic Workplace, 14*(2), 1, 3, 6–7, 14–15.

Tuitt, F., Danowitz, M., & Sotello-Turner, C. (2007). Signals and strategies in hiring faculty of color. In J. Smart (Ed.), *Higher education: Handbook of theory and research* (Vol. 22, pp. 497–536). Norton, MA: Kluwer Academic Publishers.

Tuitt, F., Hanna, M., Martinez, L. M., del Carmen Salazar, M., & Griffin, R. (2009). Teaching in the line of fire: Faculty of color in the academy. *Thought & Action, 65*, 65–74.

Turner, C. S., & Myers, S. L. (2000). *Faculty of color: Bittersweet success.* San Francisco: Jossey-Bass.

Yosso, T. J. (2002). Toward a critical race curriculum. *Equity and Excellence, 35*(2), 93–107.

Part I

Black Faculty

Navigating Daily Encounters
with Racism

Chapter 2

Acclimating to the Institutional Climate

There's a "Chill" in the Air

Mark Giles

INTRODUCTION

Through the lens of critical race theory (Bell, 1992; Crenshaw, Gotanda, Peller, & Thomas, 1995; Matsuda, Lawrence, Delgado, & Crenshaw, 1993; Solórzano, Ceja, & Yosso, 2000; Taylor, Gillborn, & Ladson-Billings, 2009), this chapter examines several layers of my life experiences prior to and after becoming a faculty member. Those experiences provided skills and perspectives on navigating "chilly" institutional climates while studying and working at predominantly White institutions (PWIs). Understanding institutional climate as social and political context offers rich analytical discourse, especially when viewed through the lens of critical race theory. Understanding contemporary cultural climates on most campuses requires reviewing and analyzing the racial history of academe. Historian Craig Wilder (2013) provides an in-depth examination of the relationship between early colleges and slavery. Wilder writes:

> American colleges were not innocent or passive beneficiaries of conquest and colonial slavery. The European invasion of the Americas and the modern slave trade pulled peoples throughout the Atlantic world into each other's lives, and colleges were among the colonial institutions that braided their histories and rendered their fates dependent and antagonistic. The academy never stood apart from American slavery—in fact, it stood beside church and state and the third pillar of a civilization built on bondage.
>
> (p. 11)

Understanding the roots of a thing helps us understand the core nature of the thing itself. American colleges were never immune or innocent to the racism, exploitation, and oppression found in the roots of American culture and systems. Viewing the evolution of campus cultural climates as unwelcoming, racist, sexist, and/or favoring the socially and financially privileged, must begin

13

with a historical and theoretical lens that magnifies light into the dark, omitted spaces. CRT offers that type of necessary lens, and knowing this history of American colleges in relation to issues of race, equity, access, and "fairness" toward all must have transparent language attributed to it. Calling a pervasive, historically grounded, biased culture deeply embedded in the DNA of colleges a "chilly climate" does a disservice to the problem and potential solutions.

The phrase and concept of "chilly climate," within the higher education context, has been around for over 20 years (Sandler, 1988) and used most often to describe the experiences and perceptions of groups of women and people of color (Altbach & Lomotey, 1991; Bartlett & O'Barr, 1990; *Chronicle of Higher Education*, 2005; Greene & Stockard, 2010; Maranto & Griffin, 2011). I find the term and ideas behind it illustrating a non-threatening and almost benign critique of pervasive racist and sexist institutional policies. It can represent an acceptable and "nice" way to say, "There is racism and sexism happening here, however, you can tolerate it." A cultural climate can be "chilly," yet manageable, sustainable, and only slightly uncomfortable. The concept conjures up images of the acceptance of certain levels of racism and sexism. That, in and of itself, is problematic. I believe it is important not to acclimate to or accept a chilly climate, especially if the "chill" represents racism, sexism, or systemic oppression. The better social justice oriented approach is to resist, analyze, work for change and improvement, or at the least, practice self-defense from that uncomfortable cultural climate.

In most of the literature on this topic, the concept connects to the unwelcoming cultural and social environments encountered by some and/or many women and some and/or many people of color in predominantly White institutions. The concept usually addresses the dearth of sense of belongingness and even the overt sexist and racist actions (e.g., micro- and macro-aggressions) members of marginalized groups perceive within their higher education journeys. My view is that the concept overly simplifies the deeply troubling and personally harmful effects experienced by some women and people of color who pursue their degrees and careers in environments skillful in the art of maintaining the status quo while making critics and even protestors for change feel degrees of comfort in an uncomfortable environment.

This chapter presents a combination of critical race theory counter-narrative (Delgado & Stefancic, 2005; Dixson & Rousseau, 2006; Solórzano & Yosso, 2002), educational autobiography and self-story (Denzin, 1989), and examines aspects of my journey as a faculty member at a predominantly White institution (PWI). The themes presented in this chapter creates a tale of self-agency shaped by my identity and role as a Black man who succeeded in earning college degrees at three top tier PWIs, which qualifies me to say something about not only my experiences but lessons learned from living and learning within those realities. The culmination of those experiences enabled me to survive, struggle, and resist within the largely White spaces that alternatively hindered and supported my professional progress.

14

Sharing stories from my journey provides insight into the ingredients and recipe for seeking greater purpose in the racially contested spaces of PWIs.

My personal background represents a critical wellspring of strength, a source of cultural grounding that continues to help me navigate White academic spaces that seek to sometimes welcome me for their own "diversity" benefits and sometimes trap me into a pseudo-reality of "post-racial" assumptions that are antithetical to the truths I have learned as a Black man in America. I have worked hard to maintain a critical social consciousness while challenging and surviving schooling processes and navigating the tricky forests of higher education (Shujaa, 1995). Learning to understand, cope with, and counter racial microaggressions (Solórzano et al., 2000) became a natural way of existing within that academic White space.

Racial microaggressions are conscious and unconscious routine, subtle, verbal and nonverbal, behavioral, sometimes visual insults directed toward people of color (Solórzano et al., 2000; Sue, Capodilupo, Nadal, & Torino, 2008). These insults have cumulative effects that reinforce the oppression experienced by people of color. Since many Whites might claim their racist actions and comments are unintentional, the injury and lasting burden of the injury rests largely with the victim. However, I realized early on in this rocky journey that I could help others who struggle within the same boundaries; I could help students, both graduate and undergraduate, successfully navigate some of those allegedly colorblind, non-racist, non-sexist roadways and byways. Because of my own struggles and overcoming certain systemic obstacles, becoming a faculty member has connected a past-present-future circle, which now offers new interpretations on my life and professional calling.

The dominant narrative of a person of color fortunate to attend college suggests that to succeed the person should assimilate to the institutional culture, work hard and believe that they will reap the rewards of their own hard work regardless of any "systemic" barriers, and never act outside the norms of the environment. The person, regardless of race, gender, or social class, will rise or fall by his or her own efforts. The institution is always fair, neutral, and open to all. There was a time, long ago, when I might have actually believed that simplistic propaganda and tried to overlook the built-in racism that awaited me on campus.

CRITICAL RACE THEORY AS A TOOL TO EXAMINE SYSTEMIC RACISM

I majored in Afro-American Studies as an undergraduate student at the University of Cincinnati. My educational experiences represent a type of counter-narrative to the master narrative of who should or can attend college. I grew up in a blue-collar neighborhood in a single-parent household (my father died when I was a small child, my mother died when I was ten years old). I was a first generation college student, under-prepared, under-performing throughout high school.

I applied to the local state-supported university not knowing what else to do but knowing I needed to do something since I was out in the world, on my own after turning 18 years old. I struggled with finances, academic focus, and motivation. Finding the Afro-American Studies classes created opportunities to learn information I did not know and that had personal relevance. I did not consider the professional paths or potential opportunities majoring in Afro-American Studies might offer.

The facts, interpretations, ideas, and theories of that discipline opened my eyes to the historical, cultural, political, economic, and systemic nature of race and racism. I learned about African history and the historical highs and lows of various African kingdoms that pre-dated the rise of European world dominance. I learned about the peculiar institution of American slavery and the more than 300 years of capitalistic, "free market" global slave trading that birthed and sustained it. In addition, I learned about the cultural psyche and normative operations of institutionalized patterns of oppression that permanently shaped the intergenerational experiences of African Americans. What I learned at the time did not make me feel defeated, subordinate, or constantly angry (although I did feel anger many times); instead, it opened my mind and spirit to try to understand the layers of conscious and unconscious actions, policies, and assumptions deeply embedded in the American psyche. The academic and cultural survival and resistance tools I learned about in college were grounded in the works and lives of people like Phyllis Wheatley, Nat Turner, Solomon Northup, Harriet Tubman, Frederick Douglass, Booker T. Washington, Paul Lawrence Dunbar, Ida B. Wells-Barnett, W. E. B. DuBois, Langston Hughes, and Charles Hamilton Houston, to name only a few. Studying African American history helped me develop a broader view of how I might operate inside and outside of academic spaces. Although I failed to achieve my potential of excellence as an undergraduate, I developed the skills to learn and have confidence in my own self-worth. These characteristics proved invaluable as I pursued graduate degrees and entered academe as faculty.

By the late 1980s, I had gained experience in various social services and community based jobs, yet maintained a keen intellectual interest in African American Studies and progressive ideas that challenged systemic oppression. That was when I first caught wind of the ideas of critical race theory (CRT). Looking back, I wish I could have not only been a better undergraduate student, but that I would have tried to attend law school where I might have learned more about CRT. I eagerly read *And We Are Not Saved* by Derrick Bell (1987) and *Faces at the Bottom of the Well* (Bell, 1992) and knew that his words and ideas rang true and connected to what I had learned as a young college student. Legal and education scholars define critical race theory in different ways. I like best the thinking and definitions of the legal scholars.

In *Words that Wound: Critical Race Theory, Assaultive Speech, and the First Amendment*, authors Mari J. Matsuda, Charles R. Lawrence III, Richard Delgado, and Kimberle Williams Crenshaw (1993) offer the following framing and definitions:

> Critical race theory is grounded in the particulars of a social reality that is defined by our experiences and the collective historical experience of our communities of origin. Critical race theorists embrace subjectivity of perspective and are avowedly political. Our work is both pragmatic and utopian, as we seek to respond to the immediate needs of the subordinated and oppressed even as we imagine a different world and offer different values. It is work that involves both action and reflection. It is informed by active struggle and in turn informs that struggle.
>
> (p. 3)

In addition, the authors provide the following six core tenets of CRT:

> 1. Critical race theory recognizes that racism is endemic to American life. 2. Critical race theory expresses skepticism toward dominant legal claims of neutrality, objectivity, color blindness, and meritocracy. 3. Critical race theory challenges ahistoricism and insists on a contextual/historical analysis of the law. 4. Critical race theory insists on recognition of the experiential knowing of people of color and our communities of origin in analyzing law and society. 5. Critical race theory is interdisciplinary and eclectic. 6. Critical race theory works toward the end of eliminating racial oppression as part of the broader goal of ending all forms of oppression.
>
> (p. 6)

When attempting to see and understand racialized institutional climates and then gauge its cultural atmosphere, we (i.e., faculty-scholars, administrators, concerned stakeholders) need multiple appropriate tools. I argue that CRT is one of the more appropriate tools available that does not allow a sugarcoating of systemic racism within higher education culture. One of the most fascinating and curious dimensions of trying to understand campus climate is through the lens and language of "diversity." First, what is diversity? Will we know it when we see it? Will we know it once it is achieved?

UNDERGRADUATE WEATHER REPORT

After earning a bachelor's degree in Afro-American Studies from the University of Cincinnati (UC), I did not have any thoughts about one day becoming a faculty member or even becoming an educator of any kind. Honestly, I was not sure what I wanted to do. I simply wanted to secure a good paying job in a profession that offered some future opportunities for advancement. The courses I completed at

17

UC and the faculty who "tried" to push me with critical thinking and standards of excellence shaped my academic experiences as an undergraduate. Yes, I resisted many of their efforts, because I had not matured into realizing the basic value of striving for academic excellence. My choice to accept Afro-American Studies as a major resulted from my failure with an initial major in Business Administration. Admittedly, I was not a "good" student in the sense of being prepared, knowing "how" to study, and it might have helped if I did not skip classes as much as I did. However, there were two negative experiences with racial micro- and macroaggressions from White faculty that opened my eyes to what a chilly learning climate in a large PWI could be. As a Business Administration major, I was required to take an accounting class. With UC academic quarter systems, there was little time for messing up in a class and recovering from it. I took seriously the advice from the freshman orientations about ways to succeed in college classes, and made an appointment to see the accounting instructor. After explaining some of my confusion about what he was teaching, I did not take accounting in high school, he plainly stated that "maybe I had a mental block related to math" and should consider dropping the class. We were not in finals week when I met with him, and cannot recall the exact stage of the quarter when that happened. Welcome to college! That was in my first quarter of college and, although I felt insulted immediately, I took his advice. By the end of my first quarter in college, I had withdrawn from three classes and earned two "Ds." I finished my first quarter (10 weeks) in college with a 1.0 grade point average.

In the fall of my second year, I took Freshman English III from one of many instructors who were on the list. It did not occur to me that one instructor was any worse or better than another instructor could be, or that one could be an outward racist. I had completed Freshman English I with a "B" and English II with a "C." The dude teaching English III actually assigned us to read *Little Black Sambo*, and to discuss its "merits" as classic literature. As one of only two Black students in a class of about 30 people, I questioned him on that idea and stated that I saw no value in reading that particular children's book in a college class. My concern was that the instructor did not want to use it as a critique on overt racist messaging in the genre of children's literature. He did not like my comments and questions. I never visited his office hours. Yet, I finished the class, did fairly well on all assignments, but was given an "F" as a final grade. I went to an advisor and then to an assistant dean, explained what happened and was told to retake the class with another instructor the following quarter. Two quarters later, I completed Freshman English III with a different instructor and earned a "B." That experience taught me a useful lesson: racism was alive and well in college settings and I had to resist accepting it, and I had to find ways to developing coping mechanisms to survive, not drop out, or not do anything that might result in dismissal. Upon reflecting on those experiences so long ago, I think my coping mechanism included intellectually checking out on some level and not consider ways to improve my focus and discipline toward excellence. As a result, I simply did a type of sleep-walking thing through my undergraduate years. I was too hard-headed to quit, but too unprepared to fully excel.

INSTITUTIONALIZED CLIMATE AND CHANGE?

Most PWIs are far less racist and/or sexist than they once were, and an untold number of "marginalized" students have gained access to and success from the wide range of postsecondary institutions that once denied them the democratic opportunity to enroll. However, all of those advancements have come from hard-fought struggles: in courtrooms, school-rooms, and boardrooms (Shabazz, 2004; Wise, 2005). None of the meaningful "social justice" advances in higher education over the past half century have been achieved through "celebrations," "galas," or "multicultural dinners." To change the cultural climate of any organization, it must result from long-term engagement to principles and policies that are intentionally designed to lead to specific or generalized desired results.

When I was hired as an assistant professor after paying my dues as a visiting assistant professor, a well-intentioned White female senior colleague offered advice. "Do not spend too much time working with undergraduate students of color," she stated. Knowing that there were few Black faculty members on campus, she felt it important to warn me from trying to help too many students who may approach me for mentoring or advising in their organizations. I responded that giving back and helping students of color was among the main reasons for me to do this faculty stuff. She acknowledged that a need is there, but I should stay focused on what matters most...getting tenure. I felt a chill hearing her words. I already had the experience of interviewing for the position twice as a way to "prove" that I really wanted it. Her words were more than a warning. Her words were a cryptic foretelling that echoed the culture of the institution, a culture that perpetuated an unwelcoming environment for students of color, and faculty of color. It signaled that I should act as an independent agent, just looking out for my own best interests and professional advancement. I was being told to ignore the potential requests from students who looked like me or were from similar backgrounds while maintaining the status quo and normative behavior of faculty. I ended the conversation by explaining that I would not have finished college if some Black faculty and administrators did not make the time to work with me. That conversation demonstrated the "unintentional" coldness of academe and the transmittance of the unwelcoming culture that has a long history in higher education.

CONCLUSION

The *Brown v. Board of Education* decisions of the mid-1950s literally altered the complexion of the body politic of American culture, but left the head, and to a lesser degree, the heart, on the same two-society track, one White and the other

19

non-White (black, brown, red, and yellow), one of "haves," the other, "have-nots." Ensuing race-based court cases throughout the 1970s, 1980s, and 1990s and challenges to desegregation and racial justice-oriented legislation have weakened and watered down many gains of the past 60 years, and repeatedly sounded the death-knell to governmental and societal responsibility to make the crooked places straight. Historically underserved and marginalized groups are currently being told to find other ways and means to navigate the historically rocky roads of educational attainment. In my imagination, I can almost hear a grinning student of color facetiously comment: "I'll have another slice of that delicious looking rugged American-individualism pie with the non-fat White-privilege topping, please." Nevertheless, when we look closely at college and university faculty ranks, for example, and who gets hired, tenured, and promoted, or who makes up the senior-level leadership (i.e., trustees, presidents, provosts, deans, and full professors) of most institutions, especially the biggest and best endowed, we clearly see a simple pattern that has been largely left unchanged. This reality keeps "diversity" programs and initiatives operational, because if all ills were truly cured, no fiscally responsible institution could justify spending any of their hard-earned and scarce resources on something they no longer want or need. Spending on "diversity" happens because blatant problems persist. My experiences as a faculty member clearly proved that as long as the conversation on diversity continues, no real change is needed, as long as I stay in the prescribed lane of not helping others too much, not questioning the system too much, I might receive rewards.

The trick bag is this: as long as institutions loudly and publicly proclaim their good intentions (i.e., diversity missions, goals, and initiatives), do they really have to show meaningful and measurable results? If so, then to whom are they ultimately accountable? For example, if your institution has had a "diversify the faculty" initiative for the past 10–15 years, yet cannot demonstrate any significant gains, although a new crop of faculty are hired each year, and if your institution routinely commissions "blue ribbon" task forces, institution-wide committees, and hires high-priced consultants, then perhaps the "Emperor has no clothes," or no one is taking the trouble to read the findings of the last few panels, commissions, committees, and consultants. More than likely, common themes and suggested solutions can be found in existing documents. There must be new socially progressive questions, thinking, and actions, and specific accountability, brought to bear on the peculiar problems of systemic racism and bias to reach the espoused goals.

RECOMMENDATIONS

- Make time to engage in self-reflection about your core beliefs and values and what you hope to achieve: gaining insight into personal vision and capacities can help guide you during the chilly or cold environments in academe.

- Develop a critical consciousness lens: engage in the research and reflection neces- sary to see and question the academy and your role in it from multiple perspec- tives (e.g., socially, culturally, politically, historically, racially, etc.).

- Do not allow fear of failure to compromise your sense of self or path to success: resist the mythology that to be successful you have to be perfect. Learn that per- sistence, commitment, and the willingness to focus on excellence can propel you forward even when naysayers who employ sophisticated and raw versions of deficit thinking try to defeat you.

- Strategically build support networks and mentors: find the networks and mentors you need to succeed even if some of those networks and mentors do not represent the dominant narrative of the academy. Taking the long view of a career, you can find several pockets of support and each might provide something of value. Make sure to find a few networks and mentors that align with your core values.

REFERENCES

Altbach, P. G., & Lomotey, K. (1991). *The racial crisis in American higher education*. Albany, NY: SUNY Press.

Bartlett, K.T., & O'Barr, J. (1990). The chilly climate on college campuses: An expansion of the "hate speech" debate. *Duke Law Journal, 3*, 574–586.

Bell, D. (1987). *And we are not saved: The elusive quest for racial justice*. New York, NY: Basic Books.

Bell, D. (1992). *Faces at the bottom of the well: The permanence of racism*. New York, NY: Basic Books.

Chronicle of Higher Education (September 9, 2005). A chilly climate on the campuses, *52*(3), B7.

Crenshaw, K., Gotanda, N., Peller, G., & Thomas, K. (Eds.). (1995). *Critical race theory: The key writings that formed the movement*. New York, NY: The New Press.

Delgado, R., & Stefancic, J. (Eds.). (2005). *The Derrick Bell reader*. New York, NY: New York University Press.

Denzin, N. K. (1989). *The research act: A theoretical introduction to sociological methods*. Engle- wood Cliffs, NJ: Prentice Hall.

Dixson, A. D. & Rousseau, C. K. (Eds.). (2006). *Critical race theory in education: All God's children got a song*. New York, NY: Routledge, Taylor & Francis Group.

Greene, J., & Stockard, J. (2010). Is the academic climate chilly? The views of women academic chemists. *Journal of Chemical Education, 87*(4), 381–385.

Maranto, C. L., & Griffin, A. E. (2011). The antecedents of a "chilly climate" for women faculty in higher education. *Human Relations, 64*(2), 139–159.

Matsuda, M. J., Lawrence, C. R., Delgado, R., & Williams Crenshaw, K. (1993). *Words that wound: Critical race theory, assaultive speech, and the First Amendment*. Boulder, CO: Westview Press.

21

Sandler, B. R. (July, 1988). The chilly climate for women on campus. *USA Today, 117*(2518), 50–53.

Shabazz, A. (2004). *Advancing democracy: African Americans and the struggle for access and equity in higher education in Texas.* Chapel Hill, NC: University of North Carolina Press.

Shujaa, M. J. (Ed.). (1995). *Too much schooling, too little education: A paradox of black life in white societies.* Trenton, NJ: Africa World Press.

Solórzano, D. G., & Yosso, T. J. (2002). Critical race methodology: Counter-storytelling as an analytical framework for education research. *Qualitative Inquiry, 8*(1), 23–44.

Solórzano, D. G., Ceja, M., & Yosso, T. J. (winter/spring 2000). Critical race theory, racial microaggressions, and campus racial climate: The experiences of African American college students. *Journal of Negro Education, 69*(1–2), 60–73.

Sue, D. W., Capodilupo, C. M., Nadal, K., & Torino, G. C. (May/June 2008). Racial microaggression and the power to define reality. *American Psychologist, 63*(4), 277–279.

Taylor, E., Gillborn, D., & Ladson-Billings, G. (Eds.). (2009). *Foundations of critical race theory in education.* New York, NY: Routledge.

Wilder, C. S. (2013). *Ebony & ivy: Race, slavery, and the troubled history of America's universities.* New York, NY: Bloomsbury Press.

Wise, T. J. (2005). *Affirmative action: Racial preference in black and white.* New York: Routledge, Taylor & Francis Group.

Chapter 3

The Life of a Black Male Scholar

Contesting Racial Microaggressions in Academe

*Ariel William Moore**

I was born in Oakland, California, in 1982 while my biological mother was in jail. My twin brother (Gabriel) and I were termed wards of the court and immediately placed into foster care. Within a few years, our foster family adopted us. Our family is eclectic to say the least, White parents with racially diverse children (e.g., Black, White, Latino, Hawaiian), as well as several children with varying disabilities. Early in life, my family lived in a metropolitan city in the Bay Area of California. In the late 1980s we moved to northern California, after the influx of drugs and gangs had begun to tear apart our neighborhood. We relocated to a small logging town in the country, nestled at the base of Mt. Herald. This town—Logginton—is situated about an hour south of the Oregon border with a population of 1,600 people, comprised of a homogenous population, mostly Whites. The landscape is accented with mountains, natural waterfalls, and endless forests. The location is so beautiful that the area is often called "God's Country" by the locals. Logginton is a place where houses remain unlocked, car doors left open with the keys in the ignition, where a handshake is as good as a contract, and where little can occur without the entire town's awareness. The town is a remnant of a lost era in history, a vestige of some of the best aspects of Americana.

However, the town is not without its faults. Logginton has a long history of racial tensions and staunch segregation. In 1909, Italian lumber workers went on strike due to poor working conditions and harsh treatment by the company brass, shutting down the company town for days. The governor and local authorities, characterizing the strike as a "riot," called in the California National Guard to dispel the strikers and the company town was placed under martial law (Helzer, 2002). Additionally, patterns from *de jure* housing segregation are still evident. One section of town still has an aging population of African Americans; this part of

---

* Denotes pen name used at author's request.

town is known to the few Blacks who still remain there as "Beaumont" (in recognition of Beaumont, Texas, where many families originally hailed) and to the town Whites as "Black town." As a mixed race person of Black and Ashkenazi (Jewish) descent (though I identify as African American), I was conflicted as a youth. As one of only a handful of African Americans in the entire town, verbal and physical encounters were commonplace occurrences during my childhood. Cottonhead! Niglet! These were commonly used references of me and my brother during my primary and secondary education. My feelings toward the town were complex, at times I felt marginalized, isolated, and unwelcome; while at others I felt a strong sense of belonging and pride. I was one of few to leave the town immediately after high school. I went on to graduate from college, eventually, earning a Ph.D. and serving as a tenure-track faculty member at a research-intensive institution.

PURPOSE

My experiences in higher education as an African American male at multiple institutions has taught me that Logginton is, in many ways, analogous to the ivory tower. Like Logginton, college and universities have beautiful imagery (e.g., buildings, art, landscape), and are rich in history and tradition. However, these bastions of intellectual advancement also struggle with historical legacies and contemporary practices of exclusion and marginality. The few faculty of color who have the privilege of serving these institutions, also have the challenge of navigating their racialized landscapes, with associated feelings of isolation and alienation. Following these notions, I engage my personal experiences in this chapter as a framework to discuss the challenges I have experienced as a faculty of color in academe. Please note that I journaled through my first couple years as a faculty member and that I provide direct quotes regarding many of my experiences, though I use pseudonyms for the names of people and institutions.

THEORETICAL LENS

Much of my experience as a Black male faculty member can be best communicated through the lens of racial microaggressions. According to Sue and colleagues (2006), microaggressions are common, subtle messages that occur in daily encounters of people of color. Sue extends that there are three primary types of microaggressions: micro-assaults, micro-insults, and micro-invalidations. Micro-assaults are explicit racial attacks that can be verbal, nonverbal, or environmental in nature. They are intended to assault (attack) people of color. Micro-insults and micro-invalidations are similar in that they are often unconscious and seemingly innocuous. A micro-insult occurs when a verbal remark or action "conveys rudeness, insensitivity, or demeans a person's racial identity or heritage" (Sue, Bucceri, Lin, Nadal, & Torino, 2007, p. 73). Micro-invalidations are acts which occur that disregard or exclude the thoughts, perceptions, and experiences of people of color. I draw from these notions in contextualizing my experience in academe.

MY EXPERIENCE

Transition into Faculty Life

I graduated from Southwestern University (SWU) with my Ph.D. in Higher Education in May of 2010. At that time, the job market for faculty members was at its worst. Nationally, faculty hires had been halted for several years; as such the few jobs available meant stiff competition among both 2010 graduates as well as those from prior years. I applied for a number of positions but only received an interview for two posts. The first interview, with a private Christian university, went well, but I withdrew my candidacy because I did not believe I was a good methodological fit for the post. The second interview was with Thaddeus Stevens University (TSU) located in Mountain Crest, Tennessee. TSU is a small, private liberal arts college located in the eastern part of the state with multiple extension sites throughout Tennessee. The institution is named in honor of Thaddeus Stevens to recognize the East Tennesseans who had remained loyal to the north during the Civil War. I was quickly hired by the university, my onsite visit being more of a welcoming party than a vetting. I liked the faculty in my department and felt like they would support my success. While I longed to become a faculty member at a research university (per my training and doctoral socialization), as a family man, I was thoroughly enticed by the offer from the provost to hire both myself and my wife (as a trailing spouse) as full-time faculty members in the Ed.D. program in leadership.

The program operated at the extension center in Knobhill during the fall and spring semesters but had a summer residency in Mountain Crest during the summer. The main campus in Mountain Crest is beautiful, nestled in the forests of the Appalachian mountains with a rich tradition and history. The area is impoverished and has a homogenous White population, many who live in the mountains (affectionately called the hollers). We moved from New Mexico to Tennessee shortly thereafter and I began teaching that summer, staying in the dorms in Mountain Crest with my wife and daughter. Given my upbringing in a mountain town, I saw many parallels between Mountain Crest and my home town (Logginton)—beautiful forests, distinct mountain culture, sincerity, and simplicity to name a few. In the mornings, I would walk around the campus and show up to the building early before class to enjoy the view over a small lake where deer would often gather. In many ways, I felt at home. However, beneath the general social and physical landscape, was a racialized climate "rife with contradictions and asymmetries of power and privilege" (McLaren, 2003, p. 69). As such, similar to my perceptions of Logginton, my feelings toward the institution were complex.

25

Commoditizing the Professoriate

Shortly after I was hired, the provost left for a new position and a new dean for the College of Education was hired. I would later be informed that regardless of the fact that I had written documentation from the prior provost of my trailing spouse agreement, that the university had decided not to honor the deal any longer. I found this information out several weeks after I had withdrawn my candidacy after receiving an interview with a top five program in my field. Unfortunately, while I had maintained loyalty on my end, this was not reciprocated by the institution. I was provided several rationales, but core among these was that the provost had not actually possessed the power to offer this deal without the president and board's approval and that the agreement was from a prior administration, thus there was no obligation on the new administration to maintain the agreement.

Complicating this circumstance was that the institution did not have a tenure system. Instead, a contract system was in place, where assistant, associate, and full professors had one-, three-, and five-year contracts, respectively. As an assistant professor, I was cautious about making waves on any issue, as the institution could simply not renew my contract for the following year. My experience as a full-time faculty in a non-tenure-track role (with tenure-track expectations) is not new. In fact, these roles are becoming more commonplace, benefiting institutions through funding and personnel flexibility. In contrast, the faculty role becomes commoditized, reducing faculty power to challenge inequities and injustices experienced (Gappa, 2008), particularly for faculty of color (Osei-Kofi, 2012).

The "Affirmative Action" Hire

While I was the only faculty of color in the department (and the College of Education for that matter), the student population served by the program was more diverse. About 40% of the students were of African American descent, with the remainder being White. I certainly felt the cultural taxation associated with being the only faculty of color, with numerous Black students seeking out my support, mentorship, advisement, and research expertise. However, as Baez (2000) has noted, this service provided me with critical agency, fueling my desire to serve as a "rock" and advocate for Black students who were problematized by a few of my colleagues. While the Black students in the program were very supportive and excited about my being a faculty member, some of the White students did not share their enthusiasm. Apparently, some of the Black students had requested that the program director hire a Black faculty member. One day during the summer program as I was walking down the hall, I overheard the director talking to her class. She remarked to the full class, "see, you told us to hire a Black faculty member and that's what we did, so treat him well!" The director was a very caring and compassionate individual, and she was trying to illustrate that she had been responsive to student concerns. I was disappointed by the comment, as I interpreted this micro-invalidation to mean that the only distinction between myself and the other finalists was that I was Black. This was the unintended message conveyed to me, but also to a room full of doctoral students as well to whom my abilities were inadvertently negated. For the rest of the summer, I struggled to maintain my authority in the classroom, as *some* White students perceived me as an "affirmative action" hire. Many tried openly questioning my credentials, intelligence, and relevance during class; I responded by being overly theoretical and using advanced terminology to try and justify my presence.

A Reverend Jeremiah Wright?

Despite this reckoning, I was very excited about the course I was teaching during the first summer. I had two sections on ethical leadership. Ethics and leadership were both topics of intense interest. Prior to coming to TSU, I had served as the co-coordinator of the Program for Policy and Ethics (PPE) at SWU. PPE was a professional development program for leaders in various sectors (e.g., education, business, non-profit, government) who were interested in advancing educational policy. The curriculum for the fellowship focused on the nexus of ethics, diversity, and leadership. Moreover, many of the ethics and leadership courses I had taken during my doctoral training emphasized the interplay between these concepts and diversity. Thus, based on this, I sought to teach about ethics and leadership but also covered topics that overviewed how diverse leadership can be considered an ethical imperative. Moreover, one primary ethical decision-making paradigm is the ethic of critique. In a simplistic view, the ethic of critique suggests that leaders make decisions that seek to advance the interests of the disadvantaged (Shapiro & Stefkovich, 2005). This paradigm has its roots in critical theory and derivatives such as critical race theory (CRT). Thus, I was fulfilled and challenged by the course schedule, even having an opportunity to briefly cover CRT in providing context to the ethic of critique.

Toward the end of the summer, I received a message that the dean wanted to see me in his office. This would be my first meeting with the new dean, and I wanted to make a positive impression. I showed up early, had researched his background, and prepared to have a nice introductory conversation with him. When I walked into his office, he warmly greeted me and asked me to sit down. Given that I am Christian and that he hailed from a Christian university, I immediately connected with him. We discussed some theology and its relationship with ontology and epistemology. After some time had passed, the conversation changed course. He pointed to a stack of papers on his desk, which were handwritten evaluations. He noted that he had been reviewing the evaluations for the program. During the summer residency, each course did not have a separate evaluation; instead there was an overall program evaluation given to students. He noted that I had been identified in a number of the evaluations, some extolling my teaching and others noting that I had "hijacked" a course on ethics and turned it into a race course. The dean noted that he had stood outside of my class on several occasions and believed that I was indeed a good teacher. Then, he said the following, "now Ariel, I want to ask you a question and I don't want you to take this in the wrong way, but it's important for me to ask." Leaning closer to me he said, "I just want to make sure that I don't have a Reverend Wright on my hands, do I?" The Dean was referring to Reverend Jeremiah Wright, the pastor of President Barack Obama's church in Chicago whom the president distanced himself from during and after his election. The dean paused, sat there quietly, and waited for me to respond. Perplexed by the question, I fumbled in response. I was fearful for my job, and more importantly for my family. I responded noting that I had dissimilar views to Wright, pinpointing specific elements of liberation theology that conflicted with my own interpretations rather than addressing the micro-insult (rude, racially based communication) (see Solórzano, 1998) that had just occurred. The longer I remained, the more commonplace such communications became, particular from my faculty peers.

Faculty Dining Entrées: Bigoted Jokes

For example, one evening, the faculty members were sitting in the faculty and staff lounge waiting for dinner to be served. There were four to five of us faculty members relaxing at the table, with a few others standing around engaged in light discussion. An older faculty member (outside of the department) and renowned scholar who was known for his jovial spirit began making jokes. This was nothing new, except that this time, he began making jokes about Blacks and then Jews. The jokes were overtly racist and bigoted in nature, and most faculty members seemed taken aback that he was making these jokes with me there. Several stared directly at me to see how I would react, while the faculty member making the jokes looked right at me as he was saying them, also to see how I would react. Another faculty member tried to change the subject; however, the faculty member continued in his conversation, seemingly enticed by angst and dissonance caused by it. For me, this micro-assault was in some ways easier to handle than micro-invalidations and micro-insults. As a more clear example of racism, I was better able to place what had occurred. I did not need to second-guess myself to determine whether I had misinterpreted what had occurred or been overly sensitive. The message from this faculty member was loud and clear, and I knew where I stood.

The "Diversity" Committee

Following the arrival of the new dean, changes to the doctoral program (and the entire College of Education for that matter) were needed. Specifically, state-level policy changes in the state of Alabama regarding public employees (e.g., teachers, principals) using degrees for out-of-state colleges (such as TSU) changed. TSU drew a significant portion of its education specialist and Ed.D. students from Alabama. In order for students to continue to benefit financially from a TSU degree, the institution would need to be NCATE accredited. The university set forth an aggressive timeline for submission of the preconditions. The dean hired another young faculty member, Jacob, as the NCATE coordinator. Jacob was a White male who had attended an HBCU as an undergraduate and was an "ally" for issues of race and racism. NCATE has numerous standards designed to ensure that colleges and education produce graduates that possess the knowledge, skills, and dispositions expected among educators.

One standard, #4, focused on educating students to work with diverse populations. TSU set out to meet this standard by creating a diversity committee (chaired by Jacob) that could discuss strategies for: (1) exposing teacher candidates to diverse students; and (2) diversifying the faculty at the institution. It is important to note that the institution had no real commitment to diversity, rather the sole motivation was to gain accreditation needed to keep the university in good financial standing. In fact, I journaled this reflection after a leadership meeting where I was assigned to the diversity committee; "It's difficult to sit here and listen to us talk about diversifying when our only real purpose for doing so is to meet an NCATE standard. For some of us, diversity means a lot more to us than simply meeting something for accreditation." This is an example of what Derrick Bell (1980) refers to as Interest Convergence, when advances for people of color occur only when their interests align with those of the dominant majority.

Prior to the first committee meeting, Jacob confided in me that he had difficulty making sure all the committee members would attend. He retorted that one faculty leader asked him, "well, is this just gonna be a Black thing?" At the first meeting, Jacob began by asking faculty members whether they agreed that diversity was an issue at the institution. I discussed the prevalence of microaggressive messages, giving specific examples and noting that I had often been called "boy" by faculty colleagues. The committee became enraged by my comments; one committee member said, "you don't know what you're talking about, even if someone had called you a 'boy', it deals more with your age than your race." She followed up this comment by stating that "you're being overly sensitive." In support of my comments, another faculty member (a woman) talked about how sexual discrimination was commonplace; she talked about how the president opened his inaugural address by saying, "some say that speechwriting should follow the co-ed rule, it's like a woman's skirt, long enough to cover the subject but short enough to keep it interesting." Concurring with her comment, Jacob noted that during the same inauguration, a senator said in his welcome message to the president, "I'm glad TSU doesn't have a bunch of international faculty who can't speak English."

29

The other committee members negated these occurrences. After the meeting, I journaled the following:

> I became dejected in the meeting, in recognition that I am the only person of color in the college, and that I shouldn't be putting a target on my back, I just asked the Chair that I be removed from the committee. Interestingly, the female faculty members whose experiences were also negated asked the same thing, at a different time. The Chair asked both of us to stay on. The microinvalidations in this environment are very difficult to deal with. Faculty don't see them as racism or sexism, but I know they are. Tired of all of this. Mentally and emotionally exhausted.

After subsequent committee meetings, the discourse had not improved and committee members had gone around to other college faculty stating that I was calling them and others prejudiced. Later on, Jacob requested that I discontinue my service on the diversity committee, stating, "I don't want to continue to subject you to this psychologically damaging discourse."

A Slave and his Master?

The dean's tenure at TSU was short-lived. He challenged the "old guard" too strongly and too quickly. He soon resigned from his post. Despite our initial encounter, I had become closely associated with the dean, likely due to my membership on the diversity committee and added role as the doctoral program director. Admittedly, I had begun to appreciate his talents, and in many ways I admired his tenacity and desire for quality. After the dean left, I was clearly worried about my position. Again, as a faculty member in a non-tenure institution, I felt that the shifting tide could easily result in my contract being terminated. I walked down the hall to Jacob's office. He was engaged in conversation with another faculty member in the department, whom I admired greatly. Seeing my uncomfortable manner and released by any tensions of fear from the dean, the faculty member said to me, "don't worry, Ariel." At first, I thought the faculty member was trying to console me, but then he followed up with the statement, "you'll be fine without your *master*." He emphasized the word *master* to ensure the message was clear. I interpreted the comment as his way of communicating my "place" in the institution. Jacob looked at me with wide eyes; he too was shocked by the statement. To this day, we still recall that moment and how we both were unable to respond because the comment was both unsuspected and egregious. I'm not sure whether I would characterize this incident as a micro-assault, an explicit racial attack but with careful undertones.

Within a few short months, I had applied and received a new faculty role at a research-intensive university in California; thus, closing the TSU chapter in my life. Microaggressions are a common occurrence in the life of faculty of color; my experience is merely one example among many on how these messages can be deleterious to our success in academe. Fortunately, during my doctoral program at SWU and in my current role as a faculty, I did not experience the daily challenges experienced at TSU. In my current role, I am at an institution that is very supportive of my work and attentive to issues of diversity. I have faculty colleagues who have helped me advance my career and engage in research that improves outcomes for historically underrepresented and underserved students.

RECOMMENDATIONS

My experience as an untenured faculty member in academe at TSU prompts recommendations for personal practice. For untenured faculty of color, I extend recommendations that may enable them to overcome discrimination. First, become aware of microaggressions – I believe my experience at TSU (though hostile) was made less damaging because of my prior awareness of racial and gender microaggressions. My awareness of microaggressions allows me to taxonomize the encounters I experienced, providing me with the ability to the name type of microaggression experienced and its underlying meanings. This provided me with a sense of power and control in an environment where I was powerless and perceived as meaningless. My experience would have been made significantly more difficult if I had experienced racial indignations and slights without the ability to identify and interpret the origin of these occurrences. Second, use journaling as a tool to release the hurt and anger resulting from hostile campus racial climates. I did not have other people of color (e.g., faculty, staff) with whom I could share my experiences. Beyond prayer, my primary outlet for dispelling my experiences was through journaling. Whenever I experienced microaggressions, I returned to my office and immediately wrote down what occurred. This allowed me to process the experience, come to terms with it, and move forward with less anger. This was essential for my own psychological well-being because I felt hatred and antipathy building within me when I did not journal. Third, publish—publish—publish. As academics, our primary currency on the job market is publications. The more publications one has (in the right places), the more likely they will be to return to the market and find a position that more accurately aligns with their values. Newly minted doctorates in similar circumstances should begin by mining their dissertations for publications. I was able to leave TSU because of my publication currency. Sometimes, other faculty of color are not as blessed to do so for lack of currency.

REFERENCES

Baez, B. (2000). Race-related service and faculty of color: Conceptualizing critical agency in academe. *Higher Education, 39*, 363–391.

Bell, D. A. (1980). *Brown v. Board of Education* and the interest-convergence dilemma. *Harvard Law Review, 93*, 518–533.

Gappa, J. M. (2008). Today's majority: Faculty outside the tenure system. *Change, 40*(4), 50–54.

Helzer, J. J. (2002). Varieties of ethnic identity and landscape among Italian immigrants in northern California. *California Geographer, 42*, 25–40.

McLaren, P. (2003). Critical pedagogy: A look at the major concepts. In A. Darder, M. Baltodano, & R. D. Torres (Eds.), *The critical pedagogy reader* (pp. 69–96). New York, NY: Routledge.

Osei-Kofi, N. (2012). Junior faculty of color in the corporate university: Implications of neoliberalism and neoconservatism on research, teaching and service. *Critical Studies in Education, 53*(2), 229–244.

Shapiro, J. P., & Stefkovich, J. A. (2005). *Ethical leadership and decision making in education: Appling theoretical perspectives to complex dilemmas* (2nd ed.). Mahwah, NJ: Lawrence Erlbaum.

Solórzano, D. (1998). Critical race theory, racial and gender microaggressions, and the experiences of Chicana and Chicano scholars. *International Journal of Qualitative Studies in Education, 11*, 121–136.

Sue, D. W., Bucceri, J. M., Lin, A. I, Nadal, K. L., & Torino, G. C. (2007). Racial microaggressions and the Asian American experience. *Cultural Diversity and Ethnic Minority Psychology, 13*(1), 72–81.

Sue, D. W., Capodilupo, C. M., Torino, G. C., Bucceri, J. M., Holder, A. M. B., Esquilin, M. E., et al. (2006). Racial microaggressions in everyday life: Implications for clinical practice. *American Psychologist, 62*(4), 271–286.

Chapter 4

Social Networking and Support

No, I Don't Know How to Play Golf

Anton Lewis and Katherine Helm

NARRATIVE ONE: "THEY DON'T REALLY SEE YOU AS BLACK"

Everywhere I go, I seem to confuse people. Walking down the streets of a large midwestern, urban city, I easily fit in until I open my mouth and out comes an accent that appears to confuse some. Much to my surprise, my Blackness seems to come into question whenever I speak. Somehow, my British accent is associated with being "White" in the United States. I seem to exist as an "outsider-insider," the ultimate *ontological Oreo*: perceived as Black on the outside, and White on the inside, a fantasy construct that actually does not exist, forced into racial reality.

I recall one of my first experiences teaching accounting classes in the United States. This was a basic course with several non-majors, thus the interest level of several students was minimal at best. We had managed to get through most of the material but only after a barrage of questions and sullen looks from my students, many of who appeared unsure that their Black accounting professor was actually competent enough to teach the subject. Students' reactions to me were varied. Some students seemed uninterested and unimpressed, others challenged me repeatedly, while others were respectful and accommodating. In a few instances, some students appeared to "act out" by challenging my viewpoints on accounting principles, speaking to my department chairperson about their dissatisfaction in the course, or simply by refusing to do assignments, citing that they did not find them helpful. Only a small number of students were consistently challenging or passive aggressive—yet this took its toll on me and the other students in the course. This experience is of course well-documented by a number of academics of color who cite student stereotypes that get projected onto them as some students discount their ability to teach (Bernal & Villalpando, 2005; Bond, 2012). For example, Asian, South Asian, and Latino professors cannot be understood because they do not speak English well enough (Lin, 2010; Rivera, Forquer, & Rangel, 2010). Contrastingly, African American professors may be positioned as "not qualified" to be at the institution in the first place, let alone teach. Indeed, as new faculty I very much needed guidance by senior faculty. I sought the opinion of a tenured professor down the hall. I wished to understand my classroom dynamics better and to improve my teaching. He entered my office and proffered these thoughts:

> "Well, what you need to understand is that these students [predominantly White] are first generation, they are lower socioeconomically and a bit 'like that'." I believe he was attempting to call the students closed-minded and unsophisticated.
>
> "Oh," I retorted, somewhat surprised by his frankness. I began explaining some of the problematic dynamics in my classroom. I asked his advice about my assignments, exams, classroom presentation, and overall teaching style. I wondered aloud why I was having such a difficult time connecting with my students.

He immediately asserted, "It's not because you are Black! They don't see you as Black."

I felt taken aback, as if someone had hit me in the chest. Literally, for a few seconds I simply could not speak. How could I not be Black merely because of my English accent? Being Black is an important part of who I am and now he was telling me that my students simply did not see my Blackness? How was this even possible?

He was so certain this was true. How could he know this? Did this mean that he didn't see me as Black either? When I got back home I began to ponder this interesting exchange. Did he mean that I am not Black in the eyes of White America? Therefore does a culture that is normatively White in fact trump the phenotype of race? Or did I in fact experience racism in the classroom that was simply denied by my fellow White male colleague because, for him, I projected a colorblind space in the class? Was it truly inconceivable for race to enter a space where culture and class crowds it out?

This curious Oreo-like existence (Black on the outside, White on the inside) allows for a different racial and cultural reality to occur, shaking cultural and racial assumptions to the core. Thus, a British accent coming from a Black man seemed to necessitate both U.S. Whites and Blacks re-evaluating, resituating, and reassigning my racial categorization as per the rules of U.S. racial existence. When my department and my institution count the number of faculty of color and the number of Black faculty, I am readily counted amongst both—however, on occasion I am not often considered an "insider" by some Black academics to the Black academic experience, though I am clearly a Black man.

I have found that my British accent seems to afford me an unwanted and unearned privilege of sorts within my professional contexts. At the same time, it can sometimes disadvantage me when I seek out my African American colleagues to build connections. It appears that "British Blackness" is perceived by many as an inauthentic form of Blackness. Therefore, am I ever truly Black here in the United States? The answer seems to differ depending on the context and the needs/motivations of others.

My "Black Britishness" has become cultural capital deployed through the notion of seeming "different" or "special." I am "Black" but a "different kind of Black." My "specialness" sometimes affords me pseudo-insider status to the privilege of Whiteness (Bourdieu & Wacquant, 1992). In the example above, because I was not overtly considered Black, the senior faculty member felt he could share information with me that I am certain would not be shared with my African American colleagues. Clearly, I was still "Black enough" for him to inform me that I was not viewed as "Black." This means that, in many ways, I am still an outsider to White World.

In essence, this insider-outsider status has advantaged me in the realms of social networking in the White academic world. I *have* been asked to play golf, go to lunch, and invited for coffee, ironically things that I was excluded from when I was a struggling Black professional in the U.K. My new, unearned privilege, however, comes at a cost. I am sometimes viewed with suspicion by my African American colleagues as they work to "figure me out" and determine if I can be trusted when it comes to issues of race. I am clear that I am a Black man and a scholar who studies issues of race and gender which is why I find it interesting and frustrating that in moving from the United Kingdom to the United States, my identity as a Black man is now questioned. I have always had a strong identity as a Black man, which is an important part of who I am. To have this now questioned simply on the basis of my accent is, in many ways, shocking and dismaying.

NARRATIVE TWO: "KNOWLEDGEABLE BUT INTIMIDATING"

I am one of very few African American professors at my institution. I am a tenured full professor in psychology and have been at my mid-sized, private, teaching institution for 12 years. Teaching is my joy and passion and I sincerely enjoy my interactions with my undergraduate and graduate students.

If one were to view my teaching evaluations, common student comments include: "she's an excellent teacher, she clearly loves what she does, she knows her stuff, she's a bit disorganized, she makes sure we understand how this applies to our daily lives" (undergraduates), or "she makes sure we understand how this applies to professional practice" (graduates). Other consistent themes include comments such as "she really challenges her students, this class is a lot of work" and "she's intimidating."

Intimidating? This is the theme that sticks with me the most. Why am I perceived as intimidating? Is this true? What does it mean to be intimidating? How does this help or hurt me professionally?

Another example of this perception of me comes to mind. After I enthusiastically emphasized a point in a department meeting a colleague told me that my "excitement" made her uncomfortable. She, in fact, asked me to "calm down" and "not get so excited." She explained that my "passion" made her nervous and suggested that I might be overreacting to the content of the meeting. Could it be that she too was "intimidated" by me? Does assertively emphasizing a point make one intimidating? Although I was not surprised by her discomfort, I did feel unfairly burdened. A White male colleague was equally emphatic as I in supporting our joint discussion, yet he was not perceived as "intimidating" or "passionate."

SOCIAL NETWORKING AND SUPPORT: SAPPHIRE AS THE ULTIMATE GOLF HANDICAP

In my discussions with other Black female faculty, the word "intimidating" appears to be a common theme for many of us. I find it fascinating and irritating that Black women in academe are overwhelmingly perceived in two different ways: "intimidating" if they appear knowledgeable and confident in their content areas, or unknowledgeable and unqualified (i.e., only in academe due to affirmative action). Why is "knowledgeable" and "intimidating" often linked when it comes to African American female academics?

This experience is both racialized and gendered. Historically and currently, Black women cannot be perceived as feminine and assertive (Helm & Allen, 2013). Black femininity continues to be misunderstood and pathologized. The "Sapphire" and "Angry Black Woman (ABW)" stereotypes invade the classroom and academic life in some very powerful ways. The "Sapphire" trope depicts Black women as overbearing, hard, undesirable, man-hating, and mouthy (Abagond, 2008). Sapphire has evolved and engulfed the "Angry Black Woman" trope. Both of these stereotypes are projected onto and into my teaching, relationships with students, and my interactions with colleagues. This illustrates an impossible double-bind as knowledge, confidence, and assertive communication consistently frame my interactions as "angry and intimidating," yet to appear unknowledgeable and non-assertive clearly compromises my credibility as a teacher and scholar. Both projections are equally damaging.

How does such an intimidating Black woman network socially and professionally and build relationships with colleagues and students? Will she ever be asked to play golf? Being "intimidating" assigns me to "outsider status," as no one wants to eat lunch with Sapphire. Smith (2003) discusses how Sapphire loses out on mentorship relationships because she is positioned as difficult, threatening, intimidating, and angry. She explores the significant price professional Black women pay, simply by being Black and female. Black women are caught at the intersection of race and gender, which compromises their social networking, support, and receptive mentoring relationships. Without these networks, Black women's large-scale

Cultural Taxation and the Over-Commitment of Service at Predominantly White Institutions

Marjorie C. Shavers, J. Yasmine Butler,
and James L. Moore III

"The popular image of academia is of an ivory tower, a place shielded by ivy-covered walls" (Aguirre, 2000, p. 19) from the demands of the world outside; however, the domain of academia has been described as "chilly and alienating" for Black faculty and other faculty of color (Aguirre, 2000). Despite its portrayal as a community immune to the problems found in the world outside its ivy-covered walls, "minority status" is used in academia similar to other social contexts in society (Aguirre, 2000). An alarming racial gap exists for Black faculty in American higher education, who only make up 6.4% of assistant professors, 5.4% of associate professors, and 3.4% of full professors, despite making up approximately 13% of the population (USDE NCES, 2010). Black faculty members are also faced with an enormous amount of challenges. Black academicians, in particular, are often expected to engage in service activities that are not expected of their White counterparts. Additionally, they are presumed to mentor African American students, serve on diversity committees, and participate in other service activities that need diverse representation (Banks, 1984).

Over the years, numerous scholars have focused on the faculty life of African American academicians (Aguirre, 2000; Bennett, Tillman-Kelly, Shuck, Viera, & Wall, 2012; Griffin, Bennett, & Harris, 2011; Thomas & Hollenshead, 2001). This body of research suggests that African Americans' expertise, talents, and skills beyond the classroom are in high demand at predominantly White institutions (PWIs). As their presence becomes apparent on-campus and off-campus, African Americans are extended more and more invitations to serve and share their expertise. The invitations magnify, in large measure, because PWIs tend to lack a critical mass of African American faculty and other faculty of color. As a way of ensuring diverse representation, faculty of color are confronted with the dilemma to accept the service opportunity or risk not having diverse

41

representation on the committee, event, or panel. Brayboy (2003) refers to this phenomenon as the "hidden service agendas." The hidden service agendas occur when African American faculty serve as the token voice of color for addressing problems related to race and ethnicity and are the identified individuals to mentor minority students.

At PWIs, high expectations and subsequent levels of involvement in service have the potential to present difficulties for African American faculty. Because faculty of color are required to still demonstrate the same rate of scholarly productivity as other faculty, commitments that pull them away from research can be detrimental (Padilla, 1994). Thus, understanding high service expectations and commitments as a "tax," an extra time commitment is on top of other responsibilities (Griffin et al., 2011). When compared to White faculty, overwhelmingly, African American faculty spend more time on activities that do not promote their professional socialization, which lessens their chances for attaining tenure and promotions (Aguirre, 2000).

The purpose of this chapter is to explore the quandary of service for African American faculty, especially tenure track, with research supported strategies to balance the academic landscape for such individuals.

CULTURAL TAXATION

Padilla (1994) coined the phrase "cultural taxation" to describe the obligation that ethnic minorities experience, due to the disproportionate representation of faculty of color at PWIs. Minority faculty members are often one of a few, if any, faculty of color in their department. Because there are such a small number of African American academicians at PWIs, they often find themselves with hefty advising and service loads (Aguirre, 2000). Cultural taxation exists in most aspects of the professoriate for African American faculty; however, it tends to be most pronounced in the service arena of faculty life. In other words, cultural taxation tends to be apparent for African American faculty. They frequently find themselves facing unequal service expectations (Joseph & Hirshfield, 2011), being overused on committees in instances where diversity is necessary, and spending more time advising and mentoring other students and colleagues of color (Baez, 1999).

The lack of representation of African Americans at PWIs contributes to the unequal service expectations that African American faculty members face. African American, tenure-track professors are often the only Black and sometimes the only minority in their departments and/or colleges. Consequently, African Americans are consistently asked to serve on committees and in areas that require diverse representation (Rockquemore & Laszloffy, 2008). Because African Americans tend to be underrepresented in the academy, these requests place a burden on faculty who are already struggling to balance the various expectations of the professoriate. The theme of being underemployed and over-used is even stronger for Black women, because they are often asked to serve in areas due to their minority and gender (Thomas & Hollenshead, 2001). In a study that compared the occupational stress of African American and White university faculty (Smith & Witt, 1996), the results demonstrated that these additional service expectations led to an increase in levels of stress and feelings, which could lead to burnout.

Cultural taxation also occurs when universities and departments use the "commodification of race or ethnicity to make an institution look good" (Tierney & Bensimon, 1996, p. 117). We can all recount instances where our names have shown up in reports as a way of documenting the institution's commitment to diversity. These expectations for service place pressure on minority faculty to engage in service, despite the fact that service can be unrecognized and unimportant in the tenure process (Flowers, Wilson, & González, 2008). The practice of using Black faculty to make the university look good while not recognizing service work communicates to faculty members that diversity issues are not valued in these institutions.

BLACK FACULTY'S COMMITMENT TO SERVICE AND DIVERSITY

Despite the unequal expectations and overburdened feelings that many Black faculty members encounter, Black faculty often express a desire to take on service opportunities and diversity work. We all agree that finding ways to genuinely "give back" to our communities are some of our favorite parts of the job. These experience help to energize us and give us purpose in the academy. This sentiment is supported in research findings suggesting that faculty of color may prefer service to the other criteria in the promotion tenure and process (Johnsrud, 1993; Padilla & Chavez, 1995). In a qualitative study of 16 faculty of color, Baez (2000) finds that faculty of color made a distinction between general service and race-related service, which was preferred. The participants preferred race-related service and found that it benefited them in the following ways:

1. it addressed their racial consciousness and met their desire to give back;
2. it provided political benefits in their racial and ethnic communities;
3. it provided interpersonal support and helped to dull feelings of isolation; and
4. it assisted the faculty member's desire to represent and advance the interest of traditionally marginalized groups.

Despite their desire to spend time participating in service related to race or ethnic identity, incongruence between the values of the faculty members and the university arises when universities undervalue these activities (Bennett et al., 2012). These findings suggest that service duties of Black faculty may include a

43

delicate balance between being overburdened and getting personal and political needs met, while also navigating the university values for tenure.

STRATEGIES TO ADDRESS CULTURAL TAXATION

Service expectations tend to be the least valued criteria for promotion and tenure, while expectations for service also seem to be the domain with the most variation within institutions (Tierney & Bensimon, 1996). There seem to be unwritten rules that govern university life that are often magnified for faculty of color (Thomas & Hollenshead, 2001). Consequently, faculty of color must approach their service in a very strategic and informed manner. In general, service is not formally rewarded, but tends to be "symbolically important" for tenure track faculty (p. 127). As Black faculty navigate the politically charged tenure process, service work can be used in a way to enhance productivity and the overall experience.

Saying No

When Black faculty members face enormous requests for service, White colleagues often advise and encourage Black faculty to "just say no" (Rockquemore & Laszloffy, 2008, p. 118). One of the authors recalls a mentor telling her this very thing when learning about her recent decision to participate in a mentoring group for minority women on campus. Although this advice is typically well intentioned, it is rarely helpful because service requests of faculty of color seem to be never-ending and because their own desire to contribute to the diverse community and issues of diversity conflicts with the act of saying no. Rockquemore and Laszloffy (2008) caution Black faculty from overextending themselves and encourage faculty to take time, at least a day, to evaluate and understand why they are choosing to participate in each service opportunity. This prevents Black faculty from making a decision without a chance to truly consider how the service opportunity will influence their own strategic process toward tenure. Instead of adopting a "say no" or "say yes" approach, Black faculty can benefit the most from taking time to evaluate every service opportunity in conjunction with their strategic approach to the tenure process.

These authors have found that candidly saying "no" has not always worked at their institutions. One of the authors can distinctly remember several instances where her "no" was not received. Because the importance of service is directly mentioned in the school's mission statement, she recalls that her response of "no" is often met with resistance and a declaration that her service on any one project will aide her scores on her annual evaluation. In order to protect her time and be selective with her service opportunities, she has found that it is more beneficial to explore why she is not willing to take on a service endeavor and, more importantly, to be able to share these reasons in a palliative way, and support them with the literature or information that suggests other ways that the faculty member can contribute.

Another way that Black faculty can resist the pressure to say "yes" to every opportunity that is presented to them is by finding senior faculty to help support and shield them. One of the authors recalls an incident where she received support from senior faculty and her department chair to help with a service opportunity. She was blessed enough to have a department chair and a senior faculty mentor that helped her to shield her service time and protect herself from the negative consequences of saying "no." Whenever she was presented with a service opportunity, she would share it with her mentor and/or department chair and they would help her to navigate the politics of saying no. One time in particular, she was asked to be part of a committee that was developing teaching evaluations for online classes. She was trying to build a reputation as a strong online instructor, but did not have the time that this committee required. Additionally, this was a controversial issue amongst faculty because those who created the original teaching evaluations believed that a separate evaluation was unnecessary. She consulted with her department chair and he encouraged her to decline, but the people on the committee ignored her and pressured her to continue with comments about how it would impact her tenure decision. Her chair overheard the discussion and jumped in and said, "I've discussed this with the senior faculty in our department and we have decided that we prefer that a senior faculty member take on this task." This took the pressure off of her and allowed her to decline without the negative reaction that is often feared.

While the support of a department chair, senior faculty member, or mentor can be helpful, this strategy must be used with caution. Faculty members need to practice declining service invitations and feel comfortable to do this alone. However, the support of others can help in high-stake situations or situations where the politics of the decision could have negative implications on the faculty member.

Aligning Service with Scholarship

When Black faculty are choosing which service commitments they will accept, choosing those that align with their scholarship agenda will help with the productivity necessary for tenure. An in-depth analysis study of 20 full-time faculty who earned tenure at a research university, and were actively involved in community engagement, found an overarching theme of integrating teaching, research, and service (Moore & Ward, 2010). Ultimately, scholarship can be used to shape your outreach. What current knowledge supports the work of your outreach? To what extent does your outreach effort benefit and affect the issue, community, or individuals? How is your outreach adapted in response to critical

45

reflection—critiquing your methods and processes and assessing the value of the outcomes? Finding ways to successfully integrate service with research can help increase productivity for Black faculty instead of serving as a competing force.

In addition to shaping your outreach, service can provide opportunities for networking across the university and college of one's discipline. At times, service may demand working with your peers around a project and/or issue within a particular time frame. Your work ethic and productivity, research interests, overall collegiality, and initiative to build bridges between your research interests and others' will expand your scholarship horizons. One of the authors served on a professional development committee across her college. As a result of sharing some hypotheses surrounding who in the college is technologically savvy, one of the authors stated, "I wonder what the data would say," and, instantly, a research project was birthed.

Mutually Beneficial Mentoring and Advising

Finding ways to participate in mutually beneficial mentoring and advising relationships is another way that service can enhance productivity for Black faculty. Black faculty members often have disproportionate advising and mentoring loads because of the small number of Black faculty at predominantly White institutions (Cooper & Stevens, 2002a; Rockquemore & Laszloffy, 2008). Helping students, both undergraduate and graduate, engage scholarship through research, publishing, and presenting at conferences will assist both students and faculty with their professional development and professional socialization.

Smith and Davidson (1992) investigated the level of support and professional development of African American graduate and professional students and found that the advisor had minimal involvement with graduate students who identified as African American and approximately one-third of students reported having no one who helped them significantly in their graduate programs. The researchers also measured professional development activities, peer network, and faculty mentoring, and many of the African American students reported not being involved in any professional development activities. The researchers found that the level of mentoring was statistically significant in predicting professional development, highlighting the importance of relationships with faculty. The enormous mentoring and advising need can cause Black faculty to feel overwhelmed; however, junior faculty can view this need as an opportunity to collaborate with students on scholarship activities that they will also need in their pursuit of tenure.

One of the authors has been very involved in finding students that are looking for mentorship and scholarship opportunities. Those relationships have become mutually beneficial and serve to not only provide the students with mentoring and the faculty member with service, but it also creates opportunities for them

46

to both create scholarship together. These relationships have turned into collegial relationships that have served to improve the academic productivity of everyone involved.

Don't Respond Too Quickly

One of the biggest mistakes that faculty can make about service decisions happen when we make quick decisions. One of the authors is convinced that she is asked about service opportunities in front of others so that she can feel pressured to accept the invitation. While this is probably not the case, the authors have found that taking some time to consider the opportunity allows them a chance to formulate a response that can be better received. The aforementioned author remembers taking some time to think about an opportunity after being approached to sit on a committee on which she had no interest in sitting. She felt pressure from various colleagues to sit on the committee and remembers responding with a response similar to "This sounds like a great opportunity. Can you please send me an email with the duties and expectations so I can make sure that this will fit with my skill set?" This response helped her in two ways. First, most people will not follow up. If they do not follow up via email, then she definitely does not take on the opportunity. Their ability to follow up helps her to get a better understanding of the expectations and gives her insight into their working style and the potential efficiency of this committee. When they actually do follow up, she can now make an informed decision. It also gives her a chance to consult with trusted colleagues and develop a response that accurately conveys her decision in a concrete and thoughtful manner.

This strategy has helped her to get out of several committee invitations simply because the individual never followed up. On the other hand, it has also helped her choose committees that align with her goals and interests. She tries to use this strategy with every service opportunity. The expectations also helped her when committee work is assigned that is out of the scope of what she originally agreed upon. While she does not simply refuse to do new tasks, she can feel comfortable asking for an extended deadline or taking less responsibility for a task when it is something that she did not plan to address. We cannot emphasize how important it is to take the necessary time to make an informed and thoughtful decision about service invitations.

Use Unwritten Rules to Guide Your Service Strategy

It is also extremely important for Black faculty to gain insight on how scholarship will impact the tenure track process in their respective institutions and/or departments. There are often unwritten rules that guide the service expectations in universities (Thomas & Hollenshead, 2001). One of the authors remembers a tenured professor explaining that faculty in the College of Education expected professors to have a service experience in the public K-12 setting. This information helped the professor to understand some of the unspoken expectations.

These unspoken rules are typically learned through mentoring experiences with other faculty. Successful Black faculty contribute their success to good mentoring, but research also shows that Black faculty tend to get less mentoring (Turner, González, & Wood, 2008). This may be discouraging, but there are other ways to gain this information. Black faculty can benefit from interacting with senior faculty and asking specific questions about the tenure process. Black faculty can also benefit from choosing service opportunities that help faculty develop an in-depth understanding of the university and how decisions are made (Tierney & Bensimon, 1996). Developing a good understanding of the unwritten rules should be an important component for Black faculty when developing their service strategies. Finding trustworthy individuals in the academy is an important component to many of the strategies discussed above. Faculty can find them by networking and getting to know others. We have also found that reaching out to mentors and colleagues in our field can help us identify people who can be an ally and support in the areas that we need.

CONCLUSION

As Black faculty remain underrepresented and overburdened in academia, our experiences continue to be marginalized. Many of our White counterparts do not wish to deal with issues of diversity because they have the privilege of not being directly affected by these issues. White faculty get to choose when to be concerned about diversity, whereas Black faculty may feel obligated to perform diversity-related activities. The journey of tenure and promotion is characterized as an "uncertain" one (Cooper & Stevens, 2002b, p. 231). Ultimately, the personal, professional, and political are interconnected. Success in the ivory tower is dependent upon one's ability to understand the culture of his/her institution and its tenure process as well as one's ability to effectively negotiate academic responsibilities and relationships.

RECOMMENDATIONS

As stated earlier, we have five major recommendations for traversing the academic landscape, specifically as it relates to service.

Say No?

Instead of adopting a "say no" or "say yes" approach, faculty should take time to evaluate each service opportunity. Simply saying no may be unrealistic and potentially damaging for tenure-track faculty, so each decision should be evaluated. Ultimately, if an opportunity is declined, as a junior faculty member, you should articulate a clear explanation of why you must refuse the opportunity. Seek out the support of tenured senior faculty to help navigate various politics and support your decision.

Align Service with Scholarship

Consider pursuing action-based research, which allows for your service to contribute to your scholarship and vice versa. Service can most certainly afford you with an opportunity to network with your colleagues across disciplines. These relationships can result in additional collaborative prospects around scholarship. Faculty members should be intentional when committing to service ventures and should choose opportunities that they can enjoy while enhancing their productivity.

Seek Mutually Beneficial Mentoring and Advising

Additionally, mentoring and advising relationships can help faculty to provide a service, while also helping both parties to increase his/her scholarship. Black faculty members are often seen as a resource and a support for other Black or minority students. This can be taxing, but faculty can find ways to collaborate with students in a way that contributes to scholarship productivity while also allowing for mentoring and advising to take place.

Do Not Respond Too Quickly

Faculty members can benefit from developing a planned response to all service opportunities. As mentioned above, a response similar to "This sounds like a great opportunity. Can you please send me an email with the duties and expectations so I can make sure that this will fit with my skill set?" will help the faculty member to get a clear understanding of the expectation. It also gives the individual time to evaluate the opportunity and seek consultation from a trusted colleague if necessary.

Use Unwritten Rules to Guide Your Service Strategy

Black faculty need to get an understanding of the unwritten rules as soon as possible. This means that faculty members should seek out advice from colleagues and find someone that he or she can trust. Oftentimes this may mean that faculty reach out to mentors or others in his or her field that they trust. Once they find someone that they can trust, they must be proactive about soliciting information and asking questions when making some of these decisions.

Ultimately, service in and of itself is not bad. Be sure that you are serving your profession, university, college, and department with passion and purpose. Here's to your successful passage through the ranks of the ivory tower. Here's to tenure!

REFERENCES

Aguirre Jr., A. (2000). *Women and minority faculty in the academic workplace: Recruitment, retention, and academic culture.* San Francisco: Jossey-Bass.

Baez, B. (1999). Faculty of color and traditional notions of service. *Thought and Action, 12*, 131–138.

Baez, B. (2000). Race-related service and faculty of color: Conceptualizing critical agency in academe. *Higher Education, 39*, 363–391.

Banks, W. M. (1984). Afro-American scholars in the university. *American Behavioral Scientist, 27*(3), 325–338.

Bennett, A. K., Tillman-Kelly, D. L., Shuck, J. R., Viera, J. M., & Wall, B. J. (2011). Narratives of Black and Latino faculty at a midwestern research university. *Journal of the Indiana University Student Personnel Association, 32*, 46–61.

Brayboy, B. M. J. (2003). The implementation of diversity in predominantly White colleges and universities. *Journal of Black Studies, 34*(1), 72–86.

Cooper, J. E., & Stevens, D. D. (2002a). The journey toward tenure. In J. E. Cooper, & D. D. Stevens (Eds.), *Tenure in the sacred grove: Issues and strategies for women and minority faculty* (pp. 6–7). New York, NY: State University Press.

Cooper, J. E., & Stevens, D. D. (2002b). Conclusion: Composing an academic life. In J. E. Cooper, & D. D. Stevens (Eds.), *Tenure in the sacred grove: Issues and strategies for women and minority faculty* (pp. 225–232). New York, NY: State University Press.

Bennett, A. K., Tillman-Kelly, D. L., Shuck, J. R., Viera, J. M., & Wall, B. J. (2012). Narratives of Black and Latino faculty at a midwestern research university. *Journal of the Indiana University Student Personnel Association,* 46–61.

Flowers, N., Wilson, S. A., & González, E. (2008). *The study of faculty of color experiences at IUPUI.* Center for Urban and Multicultural Education (CUME), School of Education, Indiana University Purdue University Indianapolis, pp. 1–48.

Griffin, K. A., Bennett, J. C., & Harris, J. (2011). Analyzing gender differences in Black faculty marginalization through a sequential mixed-methods design. *New Directions for Institutional Research, 151*, 45–60.

Johnsrud, L. K. (1993). Women and minority faculty experiences: Defining and responding to diverse realities. *New Directions for Teaching and Learning, 53*, 3–16.

Joseph, T. D., & Hirshfield, L. E. (2011). "Why don't you get somebody new to do it?" Race and cultural taxation in the academy. *Ethnic and Racial Studies, 34*, 121–141.

Moore, T. L., & Ward, K. (2010). Institutionalizing faculty engagement through research, teaching, and service at research universities. *Michigan Journal of Community Service Learning, 17*(1), 44–58.

Padilla, A. M. (1994). Ethnic minority scholars, research, and mentoring: Current and future issues. *Educational Researcher, 23*(4), 24–27.

Padilla, R. V., & Chavez, R. C. (Eds.) (1995). *The leaning ivory tower: Latino professors in American universities.* Albany, NY: State University of New York Press.

50

Rockquemore, K. A., & Laszloffy, T. (2008). *The Black academic's guide to winning tenure—Without losing your soul*. Boulder, CO: Lynne Rienner Publishers.

Smith, E., & Davidson, W. (1992). Mentoring and the development of African-American graduate students. *Journal of College Student Development, 33*, 531–539.

Thomas, G. D., & Hollenshead, C. (2001). Resisting from the margins: The coping strategies of Black women and other women of color faculty members at a research university. *Journal of Negro Education, 70*, 166–175.

Tierney W. G., & Bensimon, E. M. (1996). *Promotion and tenure: Community and socialization and academe*. Albany, NY: State University of New York Press.

Turner, C. V., González, J. C., & Wood, J. L. (2008). Faculty of color in academe: What 20 years of literature tells us. *Journal of Diversity in Higher Education, 1*, 139–168.

USDE NCES (2010). *Condition of education 2010*, Indicator 23 (NCES 2010-028). Retrieved September 7, 2010 from: http://nces.ed.gov/fastfacts/display.asp?id=72.

Part II

Black Faculty

Meaning Making through Multidisciplinary and Intersectional Approaches

Chapter 6

Black Faculty Negotiating the Microaggressions in Scholarship

aretha faye marbley, Leon Rouson, Jiaqi Li, Shih-Han Huang, and Colette M. Taylor

For Black and African American faculty, in particular, Black women faculty, *micro-aggressions*, those commonplace daily verbal, behavioral, or environmental indignities, derogatory racial slights and insults toward people of color (Sue et al., 2007, p. 271) and women are all too real not only in the classroom, but also in the scholarship arena as well. For those of us who are African American and African American women scholars and faculty, what has been particularly frustrating for us is editors' insensitivity to, and lack of awareness and knowledge of, different cultural worldviews.

These authors, like many women faculty and faculty of color, have received editorial feedback that lacked knowledge of and respect for other non-male and non-Euro-centric worldviews and frameworks, such as Black, womanist, feminist, and multicultural pedagogy, ideology, and theory. For example, the lead author once received a rejection letter from a flagship journal with the following comment in bold: "*The author failed to capitalize bell hooks' name.*"

In response to the editorial feedback regarding the spelling of bell hooks' name, this chapter, grounded in critical race and critical feminist theories, draws also from the feminist concept of *the personal is political*—meaning that the personal problems that women experience in their lives are political problems. We believe that the concept also applies to the lived experiences of many African American faculty and African American women faculty. That is, their experiences of the academy as alienating, racist, sexist, stressful, chilly, and unwelcoming are too often viewed as personal. Rather, these experiences most often are the result of methodical and systemic oppression, and, as such, become the focus of group struggle as opposed to individual struggle.

Finding a sense of academic comfort can be a daunting undertaking for Black faculty and Black women faculty, who often lack key role models and mentors to assist them in negotiating the academic and scholastic terrains. Thus, emanating from our narratives are seven of the 18 key characteristics of Africana Womanism: *self-naming*, *self-definition*, *strength*, *wholeness*, *authentic*, *nurturing*, and *spirituality*. Last, we offer two personal-political narratives on the scholastic challenges facing African American male and female scholars at predominantly White institutions (PWI) and Historically Black College and Universities (HBCUs) and a graduate student's reflection of Black faculty in the professoriate, specifically, the systemic oppression that invalidates alternative points of view.

CRITICAL THEORIES

As a concept, critical theory has different origins and histories, an origin in sociology and an origin in literary criticism. As such, in the first tradition, critical theory is an overarching concept that can describe a theory founded upon critique. In that vein, a critical theory is critical insofar as it seeks to liberate human beings from the oppressive circumstance and according to Geuss (1981) maintains "that ideology is the principal obstacle to human liberation" (p. 100). In the second tradition, rhetorical (literary) criticism, in essence, critiques the quality of the discourse (Harding, 1991, 2004; Spender, 1984a, 1984b). According to some scholars (Hall 1986; Pratt-Clarke, 2010; Sandoval, 2000), the frontrunners of critical theory were focused on the dismantling of oppressive systems as opposed to a specific philosophical agenda or a specific ideology.

Critical Race Theory

It is vital to understand that the American higher education system, much like other traditional organizations and systems in the United States, is embedded with Eurocentric values and viewpoints (Delgado & Stefancic, 2001). Because higher education in the United States was developed for elite, White men, our institutions are "raced" and "gendered." Higher education is still dominated by these perspectives while other perspectives are rarely found in teaching or research. Policies (e.g., tenure), practices (e.g., teaching evaluations), and norms (e.g., departmental ranking of journals) result in differential access to academic success and power which has been absorbed into our institutions by custom, policy, and law. This differential access can be labeled institutional racism.

Critical race theory integrates transdisciplinary methodologies drawing upon theory, experiential knowledge, and critical consciousness to illuminate and combat this institutional racism. As critical race theory points out, this institutional racism, based on White privilege and White supremacy, creates power structures that reinforce the marginalization of women and people of color (Crenshaw, 1995).

56

Feminist Theory and Critical Feminist Theory

Kramarae (1989) defines feminist theory as "A generic label for a perspective or group of theories that explores the meaning of gender concepts." Feminist theorists argue that almost all aspects of life can be understood in terms of gender patriarchy and gender inequities (Wood, 2008). Further feminist theory focuses on recognizing oppression toward women, analyzing what forces contribute to maintain the oppression, committing to reform the oppression, and envisioning the future gender equality (Avis, 1986). Whereas, Wood's (2008) critical feminist theory "Asks how cultural structures and practices shape women's and men's lives and communications practices and conversely how women's and men's lives and communications shape cultural structures and practices" (p. 326).

In short, though not limited to gender inequities and inequalities, critical feminist theory, according to Wood (2008), purposes to identify, question, expose, and reform the powers of patriarchy and gender disparities and inequities of the world, including dominant patterns and the ideologies that underlie them. For Black women faculty, critical race feminism examines issues of power, oppression, and opportunity. Black faculty can use counter-narratives of lived experiences and storytelling for making meaning of the intersectionality of not only our race and gender, but our multiple and intersecting oppressive identities related to age, income, sexuality, and ability.

In that vein, feminist critical theories were, until now, similarly engaged in thinking about the transformation of social institutions and practices and discovering new definitions of social agents. However, most recently, feminist critical theorists (Canaday, 2003; Gilbert, 1993; Kriesteva, 1986; Singh, 1997; Smith, 1982) are more focused on changing social arrangements in order to establish fairer ways in which to fight against exclusion. They are wrestling with the complexity of power and domination by analyzing the different technologies and practices and exploring more methodologies that capture the experience of women and people of color.

Further, according to de Saxe (2012), critical feminist theory as a methodology has three major components or reconsiderations for reframing and changing structures and systems (e.g., marginalization, patriarchy, and inequities) specifically in education by:

1. reconsidering our existing understandings of knowledge, power, and spaces of empowerment;
2. reconsidering and reframing hegemonic understandings of concepts, methods, and theories; and
3. the idea or act of telling one's story, and moving forward with a methodology of opposition (becomes the very essence of conceptualizing critical feminist theory).

Utilizing critical race, feminist theory, and critical feminist theory can help both African American male and female faculty embrace equity while carrying out their research, scholarship, and practice. By challenging the universality of these Eurocentric standards which describe normative measures and regulate proper academic thought and expression, these theories give voice to the diversity of voices traditionally unheard and ignored by the academy. In other words, critical race and critical feminist theories, forms of oppositional scholarship, do not accept the traditional ivory tower's perceived standards of excellence. This oppositional scholarship allows us to identify ourselves and tell our own stories through our unique voices.

Africana Womanism

Hudson-Weems (1993) defined and coined the term "*Africana Womanism*" in 1987 in an effort to emphasize the importance of self-naming for Africana women. The term "Africana" (a) "identifies the ethnicity of the woman being considered . . . establishing her cultural identity, relating directly to her ancestry and her land base—Africa" and is (b) "One in which she battle's with the dominant alienating forces in her life as a struggling Africana Woman, questioning the accepted idea of womanhood" (pp. 22–23).

Moreover, she describes *self-defining* as the Africana Womanist defining her reality and community within their Africana cultural experiences. *Strength* embraces the Africana Womanist's historical tradition of both psychological and physical *strength, whereas, wholeness* pertains to the African Womanist actively and continuously seeking completeness. *Authentic* means the African Womanist is cultural connected in her life. To be *spiritual* (a ubiquitous part of Africana culture), the Africana Womanist must believe in a higher power that transcends rational ideals. Last, the Africana Womanist is a NURTURER. The characteristic of nurturer is consistent with her doing what must be done for the survival of the family. Further it is a commitment grounded in and realized through a positive sense of history, familihood, and security.

Making it Real

I vividly remember sitting with a room full of editors of mental health and education flagship journals focused on race, culture, and ethnic issues at Columbia University to get a better understanding of why some of my best work continued to get rejected. Before the session began, I already had a mental checklist of all the dos and don'ts of getting published, and methodically checked off each tip as each editor spoke with a silent "been there, done that—my manuscript still did not get published" swirling around in my head.

Nothing new, I thought, that I haven't already heard, and certainly, nothing to explain why some of my best work did not get published . . . ironically in many of

58

those same journals. After all of them had spoken, I raised my hand and asked the question, "How do you explain the manuscript submitted from women scholars and scholars of color on those difficult topics, ones that challenge the status quo, ask the tough questions, and go beyond most of your majority readers' comfort zones, in short, make White folk uncomfortable?" "That is," I continued, "I mean the rigorous articles, of sound methodology, timely, grounded in clinical practice, within the scope of the journal, with great recommendations, grammatically correct, and follows APA and the author guidelines to the letter."

Initially they were defensive and referred back to their original comments of "following directions, within the scope of the journal, sound methodologies, etc." Finally, one of the female editors of color spoke up and shared a similar experience—then an African American male editor spoke up—until one by one each female and male editor of color chimed in. This was my first and only experience of an honest conversation on this topic.

As I look back on my 20-year stint in the ivory towers and my 40-year career in mental health, social services, and education, there have not been many opportunities for real conversations. The lyrics of an old Black gospel hymn resonate in my spirit and capture the essence of my journey with the words, "The road is rough the going gets tough/the hills are hard to climb/I started out a long time ago." Yes, in retrospect, my professional career was a long time ago.

I find it amazing (not in a good way) that in this post-African slavery, post-Civil Rights, and post-Second Wave Feminist era that I would be breaking any color and gender barriers. Humbly, I have passed many personal and professional milestones, made multiple accomplishments, and faced countless hurdles. Nonetheless, who could have predicted that, in 1998, I would be the first African American to be awarded a doctorate at any institution or the first African American female to be promoted to full professor and the only one to be promoted through the ranks in 2010 at any institutions or the first one in my community, family, and graduating high school class to receive a master's degree and a doctorate degree. It is amazing—yet the road has been rough and the going tough and the hills were so hard to climb and the compromises too high of a price to pay. Though a scholar and a full tenured professor, the academic struggle for parity and respect continues for me as a female professor of color in a Research Institution.

Nonetheless, my BFF and I decided when we were first tenured that we would write for two reasons: (a) to be prolific and (b) for impact. Though I feared that acquiring tenure would transform me into someone I did not know, we were really both adamantly committed to making an impact in our community, nation, and our world. Steeped in Earnest Boyer's (1990) mission for both service and scholarship as well as the biblical notion of "to whom much is given, much is required," we wanted to use our service and scholarship to give back, clear the path for women and scholars of color with a social justice mission, and ultimately, provide a voice for the voiceless.

59

Though the journey to associate professor with tenure was littered with challenges, we naively, and perhaps foolishly, thought the academic road would become easier when we became full professors, seasoned instructors, and renowned scholars. I am published and I still have those important life-altering manuscripts that get rejected, as evident in the scenario with the editors. I continue to focus on all of the things that were important early in my career (social justice, empowerment, my community, country and world). At this junction, I have had to double-back to reclaim, not my academic self, but my cultural self and those important elements delineated in Africana Womanism (self-naming, self-definition, strength, wholeness, authentic, nurturing, and spirituality) that I lost and forfeited during my professional career and the tenure and promotion process. When I retire from the academy, I want to exit the way I entered— authentic. That is, I want to look like someone I know.

DIFFERENT SEASON AND DIFFERENT WORLD: REDEFINING MY BLACKNESS AT AN HBCU

As an African American male faculty member at a Historically Black College and University (HBCU)—I thought life would be easy. But I soon realized that I had to redefine myself and that was far beyond just being Black, even though I thought that was my purpose in serving at an HBCU. I reflect on the lyrics by George Gershwin: "Summertime, and the livin' is easy/Fish are jumpin'/And the cotton is high." The living was not so easy and the fish were not jumping and there was no cotton. It was a different world and I had to make many adjustments and sacrifices in this continuing HBCU faculty journey.

I found myself sometimes not being Black enough, yet I knew I was Black and at an HBCU, but there were cultural and environmental values and traditions that were very engrained. Even though I attended an HBCU for my undergraduate studies, it is very different being a faculty member at such an institution. The big change and shift occurred right in front of my eyes while I was an undergraduate student at a large public HBCU (over 5,000 students) in North Carolina in the late 1970s.

While I understood the history, mission, and purpose of HBCUs, by the early 1980s the nation was transforming with Ronald Reagan as president and the HBCUs were undergoing major changes and hardships. I personally changed during that shift and I realized that the world was bigger than just being Black, but there was a big world out there and I knew I had a place somewhere in it. I had to revisit my Blackness in this new world and it ended up being at a HBCU and a faculty member in time.

When I completed my undergraduate studies in 1983, Reagan had declared us a nation at risk in an educational, global, and national security sense. I had to take a new outlook on life as a first-year teacher in an inner-city school. I had already started reshaping my Blackness. I now lived in a broader society and my reach had to reflect that notion. My parents and grandparents had grown up in the old south Jim Crow era with very limited options and choices, and I started in my early years in that same era through first grade in the mid-1960s. In second grade, I was in a fully integrated school system and it was the start of my defining my Blackness in a small premature way.

When I first started working and teaching as an instructor at an HBCU in the early 1990s, I was 30 years old—that was relatively young among mostly old to middle-aged African American colleagues. Many of my colleagues during that time were born and spent much of their adult lives in segregated schools, communities, and cities. So their views of the world were very different and often conflicting with how I saw the world and my personal purpose at teaching at an HBCU. By the late 1990s multiculturalism ideas were being termed "diversity concepts" and the big issue was not just about race, but topics like class, abilities, gender, religion, sexuality, age, language, and appearance.

The culture at the second HBCU I taught at was about family and nurturing and I deemed my role as a faculty member more about promoting and teaching global awareness and transformation. Surprisingly, my views were looked at as a little radical and even anti-Black. We (my colleagues at the HBCU) had to coexist and comprise with our different backgrounds and experiences in time. I respected my elders' history and struggle, but more importantly I respected change.

As I spoke with friends who taught at predominantly White institutions (PWIs), they had their own battles and sense of identity and equity issues—they were different from mine, yet so much the same. I was fighting for my own sense of identity at an HBCU and for my voice to be heard in a culture of pain and stillness as I attempted to get tenure and promotion.

My struggle was about positively interacting with HBCU Black and few White colleagues with conflicting views and notions in an intellectual setting yet with clear intra-cultural boundaries. I was supposed to save and protect the Black students at the institution. Yet, I felt my role was to save and protect myself and to allow my students to engage and learn in and from that process in an intellectual context. I view almost everything in an intellectual mode and not in an affective domain—that kind of thinking was not viewed as real Black in itself. These were some of my own past and current perceptions and takes as a now-tenured associate professor faculty member at an HBCU.

I have had to redefine my Blackness from not just being Black, but to being a bridge and an agent of change for all people, and in all the struggles (race, class, abilities, gender, religion, sexuality, age, language, and appearance). George Gershwin's lyrics further state: "One of these mornings/You're going to rise up singing/Then you'll spread your wings/And you'll take to the sky." Like the song, I will rise up singing and spread my wings as I move through the ranks toward full

61

professorship at an HBCU. And as I take to the sky in this complex journey, I just may have to reinvent and reconstruct myself and my identity once again.

ACADEMIC CULTURE SHOCK

I, being an international student and an Eastern Asia native, isolated from my culture, language, and family, believed that endurance and industriousness were vital characteristics to survive in a foreign land. These values and principles aided me in becoming much more sophisticated in overcoming hurdles and adjusting to academic life in the early years of my study abroad. And as such, I assumed that I could more quickly assimilate into the melting pot than my peers. Unfortunately, life is always unpredictable, even if a man has prepared psychologically and physically for it.

Let's rewind back to the fall of 2012 when I was experiencing great stress and anxiety in writing research articles. Simply put, that is, the anxiety and stress were not influentially pathological symptoms, but rather the result of academic culture shock that I had never experienced. Compared with culture shock, academic culture shock focuses on how to adapt to the style of academic research and publication in the U.S. institutes. Especially in the academic field, my professors and journal editors expected a critical understanding of the traditional paradigms and to have those paradigms reflected in my writing and manuscripts. However, as an international Chinese student, educated in China, for 30 years I was trained to be a non-critical thinker. Thus, at the onset of my scholarship journey, I didn't know what would help and had no one to encourage, guide, or help me. I felt lonely, isolated, and unable to rely on my personal principles of endurance and industriousness to cope and survive.

However, one of my African American female professors opened her door for me when I was desperate for answers. She identified herself as a social justice activist. I found her to be intelligent, knowledgeable, reputable, and genuine. Surprisingly, she was able to help me to reconnect to my principles and address the academic cultural shock. She not only taught me how to write academic papers and provided an array of scholastic opportunities such as writing, professional presentations, and grant-writing. Observing and shadowing her, I witnessed a caring person and a true scholar unlike other professors. More importantly, she role-modeled, not only empathy, but the essence of a scholar, educator, philanthropist.

Now I realize that life does not simply consist of principles and purposes, but rather, it is a long journey from *self-defining* to *wholeness* (Hudson-Weems, 1993). Moreover, we should not confine ourselves in the wall built by our so-called knowledge, culture, ethnicity, tradition, and principles. Instead, be genuine and philanthropic, regardless of whatever societal role we play, high or low, rich or poor, male or female.

CONCLUSION

How do we promote the academic and scholastic success of African American men and women and eliminate barriers of race, gender, language, culture, and attitude for the success of Black faculty and faculty of color in the academy? From a critical theory framework, we sincerely believe that academic success for faculty who are marginalized academically should begin with a critical assessment of the institution of higher education itself. That is, we must identify inequity and oppression in the academy's internal structures and systems that are upheld by majority groups (race, gender, sexuality, age, ability, and religion).

In the spirit of critical feminist theory, we also believe that Boyer's (1997) *scholarship revisited* for African American faculty compels us to challenge our existing understandings of knowledge, power, and spaces of empowerment, our hegemonic understandings of concepts, methods, and theories, and to publish our counter-narratives and counter-stories and to move forward with not only a methodology of opposition, but a strong agenda of opposition. Nonetheless, our experiences in the academy as African American faculty are consistent with the contemporary literature and research on Black faculty, women faculty, and faculty of color. Further, our experiences in many ways epitomize the experiences of so many African American faculty members in the academy both yesterday and today.

Likewise, we believe that for African Americans, women, and people of color, self-naming, self-definition, strength, wholeness, authentic, nurturing, and spirituality are the critical elements for survival in the academy. Also, identifying our social niche in an environment that does not even remotely reflect the interests of Black academicians is equally disheartening. Therefore, we believe that with a concerted effort and critical lens we can validate the authentic voices of African American and Black faculty on both PWI and HBCU campuses. Perhaps, through the writing of this book and the sharing of our personal experiences as African American faculty, we can shed some light on the cognitive, affective, and spiritual realties, and the identities and agendas of Black faculty and help find solutions to what is needed for the recruitment, retention, and success of Black folk (faculty, staff, and students) in the academy.

Ironically, at the conclusion of writing this chapter, each of us, using critical theory lens, revisited the negative experiences and factors that blocked our academic success as African American students, teachers, and administrators early in our professional career. Ironically, as African American faculty decades later those are the same barriers blocking our success today. Evident in the counter-narratives of marbley and Rouson were their ability to rediscover their strengths. They were able to validate themselves by connecting to their cultural identity, defining their own reality and cultural experiences, capitalizing on both their ancestral psychological and physical strengths, seeking completeness through

63

other venues, remaining true to themselves, staying connected to their families and their community, mentoring others, and maintaining a strong connection to God. In other words, they personified Hudson-Weems' (1993) seven characteristics of Africana Womanism—*self-naming*, *self-definition*, *strength*, *wholeness*, *authentic*, *nurturing*, and *spirituality*.

RECOMMENDATIONS

- *Be competent in traditional forms of methodologies, pedagogy, theories, and scholarship*: Though institutions are becoming increasingly open to new approaches, merit, tenure, and promotion continues to be steeped in traditional forms of scholarship and pedagogy.

- *Be competent in feminist, multicultural, nontraditional, and new forms of praxis pedagogy, methodologies, theories, epistemologies, axiology, and cultural worldviews*: It is imperative in changing the academy to meet the needs of African Americans and other groups of color as well as our nation, and our world.

- *Maintain an intellectual mode*: Think in a scholarly manner even in the most emotional and hostile situations, while trying to figure out your place in the academy (within a community of scholars).

- *Know your battles*: Be very clear about your struggles and obstacles before you fight back or attempt to become a voice.

- *Get good mentors and be a good mentor*: Mentoring is the key to the success, and it is important to remember the adage "people don't care how much you know, until they know how much you care."

In the spirit of Africana Womanism, we hope that the narratives that we have shared as African American faculty provide authentication of the experiences of other Black men and Black women faculty. Likewise, through the lenses of both critical race theory and critical feminist theory, we hope that the information gained from reading this chapter has touched on the commonalities and difficulties of understanding the lived experiences of Black faculty and Black women faculty in the academy. Last, we hope we have touched on strengths and resiliencies that encourage others to reclaim themselves and write their own counter-stories—more tools that can be used to dismantle the master's house.

REFERENCES

Avis, J. (1986). Feminist issues in family therapy. In F. Piercy & D. Sprenkle (Eds.), *Family therapy sourcebook* (pp. 213–242). New York, NY: Guilford Press.

Boyer, E. L. (1990). *Scholarship reconsidered: Priorities of the professoriate*. Princeton, NJ: Carnegie Foundation for the Advancement of Teaching.

Boyer, E. L. (1997). *Scholarship reconsidered: Priorities of the professoriate*. San Francisco: Jossey-Bass.

Canaday, M. (2003). Promising alliances: The critical feminist theory of Nancy Fraser and Seyla Benhabib. *Feminist Review, 74*, 50–69.

Crenshaw, K. W. (1995). Mapping the margins: Intersectionality, identity politics, and violence against women of color. In K. Crenshaw, N. Gotanda, G. Peller, & K. Thomas (Eds.), *Critical race theory: The key writings that formed the movement* (pp. 80–84). New York: The New Press.

Delgado, R., & Stefancic, J. (2001). *Critical race theory: An introduction*. New York, NY: New York University Press.

de Saxe, J. (2012). Conceptualizing critical feminist theory and emancipatory education. *Journal for Critical Education Policy Studies, 10*, 183–201.

Geuss, R. (1981). *The idea of a critical theory: Habermas and the Frankfurt School*. Cambridge: Cambridge University Press.

Gilbert, P. (1993). Discourses on gender and literacy: Changing the stories. In P. Freebody, S. Muspratt, & A. Luke (Eds.). *Constructing critical literacies: Teaching and learning textual practices*. New York, NY: Hampton Press.

Hall, S. (1986). The problem of ideology: Marxism without guarantees. *Journal of Communication Inquiry, 10*, 28–44.

Harding, S. G. (1991). *Whose science? Whose knowledge? Thinking from women's lives*. Ithaca, NY: Cornell University Press.

Harding, S. G. (Ed.). (2004). *The feminist standpoint theory reader: Intellectual and political controversies*. New York, NY: Psychology Press.

Hudson-Weems, C. (1993). *Africana womanism: Reclaiming ourselves*. Troy, MI: Bedford.

Kramarae, C. (1989). Feminist theories of communication. *International Encyclopedia of Communications, 2*, 157–160.

Kristeva, J. (1986). Women's time. In T. Moi (Ed.). *The Kristeva reader*. Oxford: Blackwell.

Pratt-Clarke, M. A. E. (2010). *Critical race, feminism, and education: A social justice model*. New York, NY: Palgrave Macmillan.

Sandoval, C. (2000). *Methodology of the oppressed*. Minneapolis: University of Minnesota Press.

Singh, P. (1997). Reading the silences within critical feminist theory. In P. Freebody, S. Muspratt, & A. Luke (Eds.), *Constructing critical literacies* (pp. 79–94). New York, NY: Hampton Press.

Smith, B. (Ed.). (1983). *Home girls: A black feminist anthology*. New Brunswick, NJ: Rutgers University Press.

Spender, D. (1984a). Defining reality: A powerful tool. *Language and Power*, 194–205.

65

Spender, D. (1984b). *Time and tide wait for no man*. London: Pandora Press.

Sue, D. W., Capodilupo, C. M., Torino, G. C., Bucceri, J. M., Holder, A. M. B., Nadal, K. L., et al. (2007). Racial microaggressions in everyday life: Implications for clinical practice. *American Psychologist, 62*, 271–286.

Wood, J. T. (2008). Critical feminist theories: Giving voice and visibility to women's experience in interpersonal communication. In D. O. Braithwaite & L. A. Baxter (Eds.), *Engaging theories in interpersonal communication: Multiple perspectives* (pp. 323–334). Thousand Oaks, CA: Sage.

Chapter 7

Using Endarkened and Critical Race Feminist Perspectives to Question and Analyze Knowledge Production Narratives

Natasha N. Croom and Lori D. Patton

> Some say the blacker the berry, the sweeter the juice
> I say the darker the flesh then the deeper the roots.
>
> Tupac Shakur, "Keep Ya Head Up"

In 1929, Wallace Thurman, an author of the Harlem Renaissance, published *The Blacker the Berry: A Novel of Negro Life*. Thurman introduces readers to Emma Lou Morgan and her experiences with living as a dark-skinned Black woman surrounded by environmental influences (e.g., family, peers) that value lighter skin. Emma Lou spends her entire life dealing with the devaluing of her darker skin, struggling to accept herself and hoping to one day be accepted by others. Emma Lou's mother explains:

> She should have been a boy, then color of skin wouldn't have mattered so much . . . a black boy could get along, but . . . a black girl would never know anything but sorrow and disappointment.

Emma Lou's struggle with European standards of beauty are reminiscent of some of the messages that Black women faculty receive via their graduate school socialization experiences, early career years as tenure-track faculty, and throughout their career trajectories, particularly when their research agendas promote an explicitly race and gender-centered worldview. When Black women faculty choose to pursue research that centers the experiences of men and women of color, challenges dominant notions of quality and rigor in research, and questions White-centered epistemological standpoints, their research is often dismissed or perceived as too subjective, ethnocentric, narrow, or inaccessible. Whether verbally communicated to Black women scholars or not, the subtext of such reactions to our work indicates a push toward normative standards of defining what is and who can do research.

In this chapter we introduce three concerns that have surfaced for us as we have dealt with the consequences of engaging in "darker-skinned" research agendas that have been informed by endarkened feminist epistemologies and purposefully center Black women's experiences within postsecondary contexts. We use endarkened feminist epistemology to explain how we come to acquire and make meaning of knowledge and critical race feminism (CRF) as a lens of analysis to explicate the racism and sexism that invades our experiences as Black women faculty.

Unlike Thurman's depiction of Emma Lou, however, we have embraced the notion "the darker the berry, the sweeter the root," meaning that we pursue a research agenda that is unashamedly raced, gendered, and focused on Black women. Our commitment to such an agenda runs counter to the idea that pursuing this type of work, *as Black women*, is detrimental and insignificant. We argue that pursuing research agendas from a standpoint of endarkened feminist epistemologies provides opportunities to (re)examine scholarly topics that receive limited attention, center the experiences of continuously marginalized communities, and provide alternative theories and solutions to address systemic inequities across postsecondary contexts.

ENDARKENED FEMINIST EPISTEMOLOGY AND CRITICAL RACE FEMINISM

Ladson-Billings (2003) articulated epistemology as a "system of knowing that has both an internal logic and external validity" (p. 399). Simply stated, an epistemological perspective answers questions such as "how do we know?" and "how do we know what we know?" Dillard (2000) coined the term "endarkened feminist epistemology" and explained:

> In contrast with the common use of the term "enlightened" as a way of expressing the having of new and important feminist insights (arising historically from the well-established canon of White feminist thought), I use the term endarkened feminist epistemology to articulate how reality is known when based in the historical roots of Black feminist thought, embodying a distinguishable difference in cultural standpoint, located in the intersection/overlap of the culturally constructed socializations of race, gender, and other identities and the historical and contemporary contexts of oppressions and resistance for African-American women.
>
> (p. 662)

Dillard (2000) outlines six assumptions associated with endarkened feminist epistemology in the context of the self and knowledge production.

1. Self-definition forms one's participation and responsibility to one's community (p. 672).
2. Research is both an intellectual and a spiritual pursuit, a pursuit of purpose (p. 674).
3. Only within the context of community does the individual appear (Palmer, 1983) and, through dialogue, continue to become (p. 675).
4. Concrete experiences within everyday life form the criterion of meaning, the "matrix of meaning-making" (p. 675).
5. Knowing and research extend both historically in time and outward to the world: to approach them otherwise is to diminish their cultural and empirical meaningfulness (p. 676).
6. Power relations, manifest as racism, sexism, homophobia, etc., structure gender, race, and other identity relations within research (p. 677).

Overall, Dillard's tenets make connections between one's constructions of self as a scholar within and between the communities in which we choose to engage, and the power involved in the act of knowledge production. Our epistemologies align with Dillard's tenets and should assist readers in understanding how we come to know and make meaning of our knowledge related to the issues we pose in this chapter.

Critical race feminist (CRF) theory is a form of oppositional scholarship, informed by critical legal scholarship, feminist legal theory, and critical race theory (CRT), that emerged in order to critique and replace racial and gender essentialist ideologies and practices (Wing, 2003). In this chapter we draw on two specific tenets of CRT and CRF: (1) differential racialization; and (2) intersectionality (Crenshaw, 1991; Delgado & Stefancic, 2012; Delgado Bernal, 2002; Wing, 2003). Taken from the race as a social construction premise, differential racialization is the process by which racial groups are racialized in different ways to meet the needs of privileged positionalities. Through this process whiteness is maintained as the status quo by providing limited resources to minoritized groups which causes competition and division between minoritized groups as each group attempts to redistribute the limited resources within and between groups, rather than challenging the material distribution of all resources, including those afforded within the system of whiteness (Delgado & Stefancic, 2012; Pulido, 2006). As women of color are positioned as outsiders-within and on the margins (Alfred, 2001; Collins, 1986, 2000), knowledge production from their viewpoint can be powerful. Guinier and Torres (2002) stated, "racialized [and simultaneously gendered] communities signal problems with the ways we have structured power and privilege" (p. 12). Critical race feminist scholars engage in intersectional analyses of the lives of women of color and aim to disrupt essentialist, monolithic notions of who we are, aspire to be, and can become (Crenshaw, 1991; Croom & Patton, 2011–2012; Harris, 1997; Wing, 2003). Moreover, intersectionality theory allows for examination of interlocking systems of oppression when multiplicative marginalized identities exist (Collins, 2000; Crenshaw, 1991; hooks, 1981).

GETTING TO THE ROOTS

Thurman's depiction of Emma Lou's story is quite compelling as light-/dark-skinned narratives are still relevant today. In this section we will "raise some important questions about the control and production of knowledge – particularly knowledge about people and communities of color" (Ladson-Billings, 2003, p. 272). We center our dialogues on three metaphoric examples that stem from our personal experiences and observations: (1) *Academic Haterism*; (2) the *Bo Derek Effect*; and (3) the *Black Male Fetish*.

Academic Haterism

Academic haterism is likened to intraracial discrimination or colorism. It occurs when (metaphorically) lighter-skinned Black people discriminate against darker-skinned Black people. We have both witnessed this phenomenon in similar and different ways given our past and current positions in academe and the professoriate. Some questions we pose related to academic haterism are: (1) in what ways are we socializing graduate students and faculty to be academic haters; (2) how do we create scholarly communities driven by collaboration as opposed to unhealthy competition; and (3) what role does competition serve in scholarly communities of color?

Socialization is the process by which one learns norms, values, and behaviors within a specific context (e.g., doctoral education, tenure-track faculty, researcher) (Austin, 2002). Within our own mentor–mentee relationship, we understand that there are dominant approaches to being tenure-track and tenured faculty that existed well before we enter into the professoriate. For example, the act of constructing a scholarly identity and research agenda can be viewed from dominant views of knowledge construction, which would be built on an individualist, meritocratic perspective. As women operating from endarkened feminist epistemologies we would suggest that scholarly identities and research agendas get constructed within and across communities. In academic spaces (e.g., professional conferences), there seems to be a great deal of academic haterism occurring, particularly between and within communities of color. While we both have connected with great colleagues, it is disheartening to see less intentionality about working together, particularly when the work is complementary, citing each other's work, and socializing new, up-and-coming scholars within our communities. The climate of the professoriate drives this type of behavior as it promotes division rather than collaboration. Such patterns can be seen in the tenure process. For example, advice to junior faculty related to publishing usually includes phrases like "keep your head down and publish" and "don't get involved in the community or with too much service or outreach." Further, in the tenure evaluation process, value is placed on single- or lead-author publications in "top" journals rather than collaborative work in publication venues that serve more than just those in academe.

We are not arguing that competition is solely negative; however, as communities that are marginalized in higher education we question the cost of competition and how it drives some scholars of color to engage in marginalization and maintain oppressive systems against their counterparts. Differential racialization might serve as a way to analyze this concern. Consider this: academe and the professoriate maintain competition for resources within communities of color in ways that fail to address the larger inequities that are happening throughout academe. For example, we should question who funds what scholarship and why. Whose scholarship gets published, where, and why (see Stanley, 2007)? More explicitly, we should question how some of our scholarship gets labeled, valued, and used to position other research as irrelevant. Messages that have been sent to us as scholars engaged in research that centers the experiences of Black women and seeks to disrupt oppressive systems and behaviors include: "there's limited funding for *your kind of research*," "only certain publications take *your kind of research*" (both comments made directly to us), and "in *your kind of research* you should focus on identifying barriers for your participants and the tools they used to overcome them" (written feedback on a rejected manuscript from a top-tier journal). These messages suggest that there are limited outlets and sources of support for such critical scholarship. These perspectives are maintained through academic haters who perpetuate internalized dominant ideologies of epistemology and academic culture thus maintaining silos within and between communities of scholars of color because they may be more concerned with conforming to advance their own agendas.

The Bo Derek Effect

The Bo Derek Effect happens when White European features are positioned as the ultimate standard of beauty. Bo Derek became famous in the movie *10* and, in a single moment, she captured national acclaim as the standard of beauty (e.g., White, thin, blond, etc.). The fact that she did it in cornrows, a hairstyle traditionally associated with Black women communities, ushers in another set of issues. Questions we raise related to the issues the Bo Derek Effect elicit include: (1) what role do the margins play in the lives of Black women scholars and can

71

they be repurposed; (2) how does continuously situating Black women scholars, and other women of color scholars, on the margins contribute to the co-opting of knowledge produced by those communities; and (3) what happens to critical research from communities of women scholars of color when it is co-opted by other communities of scholars?

Whether in society at large or in academe specifically, Black women scholars are rarely, if ever, considered to be the standard. Moreover, the work we generate can be so easily co-opted. Take, for example, Kimberlé Crenshaw (1991) and Patricia Collins' (2000) work on intersectionality. These works speak to occupying multiple marginalities at the individual and intra/interpersonal levels, as well as the multiplicative, as opposed to additive, effects of multiple marginalized positionalities within macro-systems of domination and oppression. What is becoming problematic is the manner in which intersectionality theory has been shifted and likened to scholarship on multiple identities, which acknowledges the possession of many identities and the salience of said identities in particular contexts but is not concerned with the structural determinants of inequality and how they disproportionately affect women of color. This co-opting results in the theoretical erasure of women of color (Crenshaw, 1991), meaning if intersectionality and multiple identity theories become synonymous the original premise and relevance of the former is lost. By transforming the discourse of intersectionality to align more closely with multiple identity theory it depoliticizes intersectionality and removes the macro-level implications related to power, privilege, and systems of oppression that intersectional theorists are attempting to assert. Therefore, in order to truly engage in that work, all parties would need to consider that:

> Feminists of color assume that the construction of knowledge is about power—not only to construct discourse but also to justify or leave untouched the material basis for the distribution of power. Consequently, eternal deconstruction inevitably (whether inadvertently or not) leads to maintaining the status quo.
>
> (Hurtado, 2003, p. 219)

Intersectionality theory is but one example and can be seen across the academy, particularly when some White scholars take up research pertaining to Black communities. When we engage in this research, we are viewed as too subjective or close to the issue, whereas when our White, and particularly White women, colleagues take up the issue they are seen as objective and having insights that make their work the standard—despite years of work contributed by women scholars of color in those areas (see Delgado Bernal & Villalpando, 2002).

Additionally, the Bo Derek Effect contributes to the discourse that consistently positions Black women faculty as academic "help" or the "maids of academe" (Harley, 2008). Specifically, our contributions to our departments are often centered on teaching and service. While both are important we should not be relegated to these areas only to the detriment of our research interests. Some examples include being asked to teach diversity related courses as opposed to other courses in which we are capable of demonstrating expertise, being asked to chair major committees (e.g., departmental or college level) pre-tenure, or being persuaded to accept large-scale administrative responsibilities (e.g., program coordination, department chair) prior to promotion to full professor. These examples demonstrate the lived experiences of many Black women faculty who are ushered toward service and teaching to the detriment of their research. Sometimes the lack of focus on research leaves our scholarship susceptible to co-optation by others.

The Black Male Fetish

The Black Male Fetish is our way of capturing gender privilege among Blacks in the academy. Gender privilege mediates how Black men and women fare in comparison to and against one another in academe. There is no question that the most pressing issues of the day are Black men's experiences in education (coupled overall with the experiences of men of color in postsecondary contexts). Questions that we raise here include: (1) what role does gender play in how research agendas get constructed and supported within Black communities of scholars; and (2) how do current narratives of Black men's experiences in higher education contribute to the new constructions of narratives about Black females in higher education?

There is consistent negotiation of politics when doing critical, explicitly raced work in spaces that reinforce the notion that such scholarship is antithetical to the interests of funders and mainstream audiences. The margins have not only meant negotiating margin–mainstream but also negotiating margin–margin. Given a desire to illuminate the experiences of Black women in our scholarship, we have found that such scholarship is deemed unimportant and irrelevant, particularly in comparison to the scholarship on Black men, much of which is grounded in comparison to Black women. It is difficult to garner the interests of publishers or funders in work on Black college women because feedback often suggests that, while interesting, books on Black women are less likely to interest readers and could result in low sales.

The importance and placement of Black men's voices and experiences over Black women certainly has historical precedence, but within the past decade the interest in Black men has catapulted. For example, the George Zimmerman verdict prompted President Obama to publicly discuss the challenges facing Black boys and men, further pushing their issues into the public conscience. Additionally, President Obama's "My Brother's Keeper" initiative (http://www.whitehouse.gov/my-brothers-keeper, 2014) and recent articles in well-read journals such as *Diverse Issues* (see Watson, 2012) have continued to force Black male issues to the forefront, causing research on Black men to more likely be funded, published, and rewarded in myriad ways. This is a good thing, and we argue that even more needs to be done in terms of learning how Black men experience life within and beyond the academy. Unfortunately, much of this work fuels a narrative of invisibility for Black women. Theodore Johnson (2013), a contributor for thegrio.com posted an opinion piece titled, "The Reality of Black Male Privilege" and articulates how the issues Black men endure become the issues all Black people face. He notes, "black women [are] either serving as props in narratives about black men, or being left out altogether" (para. 8). Similarly, Dr. Lori Patton was quoted by Stacey Patton (2012) in an article in the *Chronicle of Higher Education*, stating, "As the literature positions black men as disappearing from the educational pipeline, black women are rarely even acknowledged as part of the pipeline, and when they are, their experiences are used to make a point about black men" (para. 26).

The current discourse related to Black women is also driven by comparisons to Black men. Apparently, Black women are the new model minority according to Kaba (2008). The model minority myth is a tool of differential racialization (Pulido, 2006) that treats Black women as a monolithic group, dismisses the impact of overarching systems of oppression that remain present in our lives, suggests that we live a problem-free existence, ignites "superwoman" stereotypes and discredits the need for the centering of our voices in scholarship furthering contributing to sustained invisibility. The appropriation of this caricature on Black women presumes a "successful black women" narrative that is numerically driven by matriculation and degree attainment data comparing Black men and women, as well as dominant Black men narratives. However, the model minority myth applied to Black women ignores their actual experiences, particularly the reality that many Black women may be "succeeding" *in spite* of rather than *because of*. More specifically, this narrative promotes greater invisibility, leaving systemic issues unchallenged. Further, whether acknowledged or not, the "successful" Black woman narrative continues to silence conversations about intersectionality, multiple marginalized identities, and the maintenance of oppressive and marginalizing systems.

RECOMMENDATIONS

Above we presented three separate but interconnected narratives, Academic Haterism, the Bo Derek Effect, and the Black Male Fetish, which have influenced our experiences as Black women in the academy. We posed some enduring questions and discussed them using endarkened and critical race feminist perspectives. In this section we offer recommendations based on the ideas we presented in this chapter.

Academic Haterism

■ Don't be an academic hater because there are too few scholars of color doing critical work in the academy. It is incumbent upon us to support each other's work in as many ways as possible. For example, citing one another's work increases the influence and reach of written work. These practices can begin in graduate school with socialization processes.

■ Don't hate. Collaborate! Make concerted efforts to collaborate with others. Doing so affords opportunities to engage in scholarly activities that enhance rather than diminish each other's work. Also, assign colleagues' work in your courses, invite them to help create or join existing research teams, and celebrate colleagues' work via social media. These techniques can influence and build healthy scholarly communities and celebrate accomplishments.

■ Hating often starts from within; therefore we must begin with engaging in a process of reflexivity and creating a mindset oriented toward community building and uplift rather than competition. This process can disrupt ideas and practices that often emerge among racially and ethnically oppressed groups who have been convinced by larger systems of domination that resources are so limited that we must hurt each other and compete with one another as opposed to working collectively to dismantle oppressive systems in the academy.

The Bo Derek Effect

■ Work the margins. While the Bo Dereks of the world may hold center stage at times, the margins are still an influential place to be. Critical theories such as intersectionality, Black feminist thought and endarkened feminist epistemologies help us all to consider the depth of issues and their implications for diverse populations. More importantly, such perspectives are valuable because they are informed by the effects of having lived at the convergence of multiple marginalized identities. Rather than denigrate the work of women scholars of color because it emerges from the margins, it is important to recognize it as a site of strength and resistance.

■ Avoid co-opting the work of women scholars of color. By being explicit and intentional about the history of the work and the people who have moved it forward, those who use the work of women scholars of color are demonstrating respect and appreciation of the origins of such work. For example, intersectionality theory should be used to address systems of oppression and the domination that ensues. Though influential on other emergent ideas (i.e., multiple dimensions of identity theory), intersectionality should not be situated as a conflated or catch-all term to capture these ideas. Doing so dismisses the original work and deprives it of its power and momentum, leaving intersectionality open to co-optation.

75

■ Scholars with more privileged positionalities should be mindful of co-opting the work of scholars of color. Research is not apolitical and knowledge production is not objective. In a community of scholars, we each should be aware of our role in knowledge production and how we can move scholarship forward without further marginalizing and oppressing other scholars in that community.

The Black Male Fetish

■ Situate research on men of color within the scholarship on men to acknowledge the impact of gender and race more accurately. Avoid a zero-sum game and the ever-present *oppression Olympics* that is detrimental for both Black men and women. Positioning Black women as model minorities, for example, only fuels rifts within Black communities.

■ Those doing the important work about men of color must be cognizant of the effect this scholarship may have on the work about women of color and be willing to address the effects in public ways.

■ When using critical-oriented pedagogies and theories, such as critical race theory or intersectionality theory, in research processes and recommendations, scholars should acknowledge differences between oppressed and privileged racialized and gendered converging identities.

CONCLUSION

Through our use of endarkened feminist epistemological and critical race feminist perspectives we have provided some interpretations of our experiences in academe. We hope the three themes above, constructed as *Academic Haterism*, the *Bo Derek Effect*, and the *Black Male Fetish*, begin and continue conversations on compelling issues that call for diverse epistemological and analytical interpretations. Ladson-Billings (1997) stated:

> The academy is shaped by many social forms. More women of color are defining and redefining their roles within it. New ways of thinking about teaching and research have provided spaces for [us] to challenge old assumptions about what it means to be in the academy . . . new paradigms emerging from black women's scholarship provide me with a liberatory lens through which to view and construct my scholarly life.
>
> (p. 66)

Endarkened feminist epistemologies and critical race feminism have served to sustain us in our academic careers and push us toward aspirations of career advancement despite the hegemonic realities that remain largely uninterrupted. Through the collective works of scholars such as Dillard, Collins, Crenshaw, and hooks, we have come to conceptualize the margins not only as a space in which one has been sidelined and relegated, but also as a space where one can feel centered and engage in work that preserves us mentally, emotionally, spiritually, and psychologically. Endarkened feminist epistemological and critical race feminist perspectives help us to see and articulate how power is situated in our research agendas and in our roles as faculty members. These perspectives also lead us to continue questioning the academy and the ways privilege and oppression get reproduced as we see it happen over and over again. We hope our questions lead to acts that disrupt, deconstruct, construct, and repurpose.

REFERENCES

Alfred, M. V. (2001). Expanding theories of career development: Adding the voices of African American women in the White academy. *Adult Education Quarterly, 51*(2), 108–127.

Austin, A. E. (2002). Preparing the next generation of faculty: Graduate school as socialization to the academic career. *Journal of Higher Education, 73*(1), 94–122.

Collins, P. H. (1986). Learning from the outsider within: The sociological significance of Black feminist thought. *Social Problems, 33*(6), S14–S32.

Collins, P. H. (2000). *Black feminist thought: Knowledge, consciousness, and the politics of empowerment* (2nd ed.). New York, NY: Routledge.

Crenshaw, K. (1991). Mapping the margins: Intersectionality, identity politics and violence against women in color. *Stanford Law Review, 43*(6), 1241–1299.

Croom, N. N., & Patton, L. D. (2011–2012). The miner's canary: A critical race perspective on the representation of black women full professors. *Negro Educational Review, 62–63*(1–4), 13–39.

Delgado, R., & Stefancic, J. (2012). *Critical race theory: An introduction* (2nd ed.). New York, NY: New York University.

Delgado Bernal, D. (2002). Critical race theory, Latino critical theory, and critical raced-gendered epistemologies: Recognizing students of color as holders and creators of knowledge. *Qualitative Inquiry, 8*(1), 105–126.

Delgado Bernal, D., & Villalpando, O. (2002). An apartheid of knowledge in academia: The struggle over the "legitimate" knowledge of faculty of color. *Equity & Excellence in Education, 35*(2), 169–180.

Dillard, C. B. (2000). The substance of things hoped for, the evidence of things not seen: Examining an endarkened feminist epistemology in educational research and leadership. *International Journal of Qualitative Studies, 13*(6), 661–681.

Guinier, L., & Torres, G. (2002). *The miner's canary: Enlisting race, resisting power, transforming democracy*. Cambridge, MA: Harvard University.

Harley, D. A. (2008). Maids of academe: African American women faculty at predominately white institutions. *Journal of African American Studies, 12*, 19–36.

Harris, A. P. (1997). Race and essentialism in feminist legal theory. In A. K. Wing (Ed.), *Critical race feminism: A reader* (pp. 11–17). New York, NY: New York University Press.

hooks, b. (1981). *Ain't I a woman: Black women and feminism.* Boston, MA: South End.

Hurtado, A. (2003). Theory in the flesh: Toward an endarkened epistemology. *International Journal of Qualitative Studies in Education, 16*(2), 215–225.

Johnson, T. (2013, August 30). The reality of black male privilege [Web log post]. Retrieved April 9, 2014 from: http://thegrio.com/2013/08/30/the-reality-of-black-male-privilege/.

Kaba, A. J. (2008). Race, gender, and progress: Are Black American women the new model minority? *Journal of African American Studies, 12*(4), 309–335.

Ladson-Billings, G. (1997). For colored girls who have considered suicide when the academy's not enough: Reflections of an African American woman scholar. In A. Neumann, & P. Peterson (Eds.), *Learning from our lives: Women, research, and autobiography in education* (pp. 52–70). New York, NY: Teachers College, Columbia University.

Ladson-Billings, G. (2003). Racialized discourses and ethnic epistemologies. In N. K. Denzin, & Y. S. Lincoln (Eds.), *The landscape of qualitative research* (2nd ed., pp. 398–432). Thousand Oaks, CA: Sage.

Palmer, P. M. (1983). White women/Black women: The dualism of female identity and experience in the United States. *Feminist Studies, 9*(1), 151–170.

Patton, S. (2012, October 29). From cellblock to campus, one black man defies data. *Chronicle of Higher Education.* Retrieved April 9, 2014 from: http://chronicle.com/article/In-Terms-of-Gender/135294/.

Pulido, L. (2006). *Black, brown, yellow, and left: Radical activism in Los Angeles.* Los Angeles: University of California.

Stanley, C. A. (2007). When counter narratives meet master narratives in the journal editorial review process. *Educational Researcher, 36*(1), 14–24.

Thurman, W. (1929). *The blacker the berry: A novel of negro life.* New York, NY: Simon & Schuster.

Watson, E. (2012). Black men face cycle of hostility, vulnerability and victimization. Retrieved August 19, 2014 from: diverseeducation.com/article/49970.

Wing, A. K. (Ed.). (2003). *Critical race feminism: A reader* (2nd ed.). New York, NY: New York University.

Chapter 8

Navigating Race-Gendered Microaggressions

The Experiences of a Tenure-Track Black Female Scholar

Dorinda J. Carter Andrews

> I am struck by my lived contradiction: To be a professor is to be an anglo; to be a Latina is not to be an anglo. So how can I be both a Latina and a professor? To be a Latina professor, I conclude, means to be unlike and like me. Que locura! What madness! . . . As Latina professors, we are newcomers to a world defined and controlled by discourses that do not address our realities, that do not affirm our intellectual contributions, that do not seriously examine our worlds. Can I be both Latina and professor without compromise?
>
> (Alemán, 1995, pp. 74–75)

Can I be a Black female and a scholar without compromise? Indeed to be a Black female scholar in the academy means to be unlike and like me. Alemán's words above poignantly describe the sometimes overwhelming task of negotiating multiple identities as a professor of color in ways that are (de)humanizing and self-preserving while progressing toward tenure. There is a solid and growing body of research that explores the lived experiences of female faculty of color in higher education. Although several scholars have written about the experiences of Black female professors in the academy (Boyd, Cintrón, & Alexander-Snow, 2010; Gregory, 2001; Harris, 2007; Patton, 2004; Stanley, 2006; Thomas & Hollenshead, 2001; Tillman, 2012; Turner & Meyers, 2000), there is still much to uncover about the raced-gendered experiences of these women, particularly in predominantly White institutions (PWIs).

Black female faculty in PWIs are challenged with having to develop an arsenal of emotional and psychological weaponry against the cumulative effects of the gendered racism and racist sexism that many of us experience. Smith and colleagues best describe this challenge as racial battle fatigue (Smith, Yosso, & Solórzano, 2006). Undoubtedly, as a Black female scholar, resisting the hegemonic normative construction of what it means to be a scholar often results in *gendered racial battle fatigue*. As women of color in the academy we experience frequent racial and gender macro- (institutional and systemic) and micro- (individual and class-room) aggressions that serve as gentle reminders that "a real scholar" is White, male, and often embodies an oppressive epistemological approach to research, teaching, and service. Our daily struggle against these assaults carries emotional, physical, and psychological costs (Gregory, 2001). Consequently for the Black female scholar who is also non-tenured, issues of identity and power pose serious threats to success in the academy.

In this chapter, I describe some of the challenges I faced as a tenure-track assistant professor in a research-intensive PWI. I am currently an associate professor with tenure. I utilize the racial microaggressions concept and Black feminist thought (BFT) to examine two aspects of the double jeopardy that Black female professors experience in the academy: the raced-gendered challenges with legitimation as a scholar and existence as an "insider-outsider" (Collins, 1991/2008) in my department. As Collins (1996) states, being a racialized woman in a PWI requires one embody a stream of consciousness and awareness of oneself as the proverbial other. I discuss my experiences with what I call inclusive exclusion as part of the double jeopardy that some Black female faculty experience as a result of the enactment of our racial and gender identities in PWIs. Through an examination of my experiences, I highlight the ways in which raced-gendered experiences serve to further marginalize and isolate female faculty of color through experiences with racial micro- and macroaggressions in the academy. "If we ignore the narratives of faculty of color and do not listen to and learn from their experiences to effect institutional change in meaningful ways, this could have a profound impact on the recruitment and retention of faculty of color in higher education" (Stanley, 2006, p. 708). In the collective struggle for justice, love, and peace, I strive to maintain my existence within the academy while simultaneously mentoring a future cadre of Black female scholars.

RACIAL MICROAGGRESSIONS AND BLACK FEMINIST THOUGHT AS THEORETICAL LENSES

Racial microaggressions are defined as subtle verbal, nonverbal, and/or visual insults directed toward African Americans and other people of color, often unintentionally and unconsciously (Davis, 1989; Pierce, Carew, Pierce-Gonzalez, & Wills, 1978; Solórzano, Ceja, & Yosso, 2000). For Black female faculty, these insults are attacks on our identities based on misguided assumptions and stereotypes about our racial and gender group statuses in society and in the academy as intellectually inferior to a dominant racial and gender group (in this case White males). As Black female faculty we often experience a double oppression due to the cultural markers of our race and gender (Harris, 2007). Black feminist theory allows me to capture my unique experiences and position as a Black woman in a PWI by recognizing the oppressive nature of gender construction and of race construction interacting simultaneously to further marginalize me as a scholar. My experiences differ from those of White female faculty in the academy, who may experience similar gender microaggressions but do not contend with the added layer of racism under White supremacy.

AIN'T I A SCHOLAR? LEGITIMATION STRUGGLES

Constantly countering the dominant construction of what it means to be a scholar bears psychic taxation—it is part of the racial battle fatigue that I experience in higher education. For many Black female professors, this battle fatigue occurs in relationships with colleagues and through lack of validation of one's research and scholarship. This is a common finding in existing literature by and about Black women faculty and other faculty of color (Stanley, 2006; Thomas & Hollenshead, 2001). Here I describe two experiences with issues of legitimation on my tenure journey. One distinct challenge with legitimation as a Black female scholar manifested itself through my relationship with my teaching mentor. When I arrived as a new faculty member in my department, I was able to select a scholarship mentor and a teaching mentor. My teaching mentor, Dan,[1] was a middle-aged White male who had been a faculty member in the department for a long time and was nearing retirement. Along with several other doctoral students, I was going to be teaching the undergraduate social foundations course that Dan had been coordinating and teaching for many years. Dan was very instrumental in helping me learn the technical procedures for the course as well as mastering the content and array of instructional strategies that had been used for the course. We had a solid working relationship; however, our relationship was challenged by the fact that Dan liked to refer to me as "girl" as what I assumed was supposed to be a term of endearment. Being new to the department and in my first year as a tenure-track faculty member, I wasn't quite sure how to approach Dan about this manner of reference for me. If Dan saw me in the halls, he would say, "Well, hey girl!" or if we were having a conversation in his office, he would use the term "girl" throughout the conversation. While I think Dan viewed this term as his way of culturally connecting with me, I found it offensive and unprofessional.

I recall an instance when I was in a meeting with Dan and two White female colleagues. The meeting had not officially begun, and there was informal conversation taking place. I was talking to my female colleagues when Dan wanted to speak. He looked at me, slammed his hand down on the conference table and said, "Now shut up girl, and listen!" Dan's tone was not angry; rather, he spoke jokingly. But I did not find his behavior or words to be funny at all. My other two

---

1 All names are pseudonyms.

colleagues (who were both tenured White females) had no words of scolding for Dan at the time of the incident and no words of comfort for me after the meeting. In fact, the meeting began shortly thereafter as if everything was business as usual.

To add fuel to this growing fire, I became pregnant during the same academic year. Once the pregnancy became noticeable, Dan asked me if I was expecting a child. When I told him yes, he said in his joking voice again, "Well, damn, girl, are you married?" As if the blatant sexism and overt disrespect was not enough, Dan posed his question loudly in a public office area. I was angered that he had the audacity to ask me about my marital status and simultaneously embarrassed, hoping that no one sitting in their office heard him. It seemed that in Dan's mind pregnancy and marriage were linked; surely his female faculty colleague would not be having a baby out of wedlock! After consulting with trusted internal and external mentors, I decided to speak with Dan about my growing irritation with his lack of professionalism and disrespect toward me. In a phone conversation, I proceeded to remind Dan of these incidences and my disappointment with his behavior. Instead of being apologetic and figuring out how we could move forward in a healthy working relationship, Dan commenced to reverse the situation and talk about times that he felt I had disrespected him in public spaces. Before I knew it, I found myself apologizing to Dan! He had managed to deflect his discriminatory behavior onto me as a way to preserve his power and domination.

My relationship with Dan, while quite helpful in my early years as an assistant professor, was also challenged by me being on the receiving end of several racial and gender microaggressions committed by him. Dan's perception of me as his "girl" who might be carrying a bastard baby exacerbated the denigration I experienced in public (meetings) and private (his office) professional spaces. In her discussion of the challenges Black female scholars in educational leadership face, Linda Tillman (2012) beautifully captures what my experience with Dan mirrors by stating, "I should be courteous enough to allow whites to not only marginalize me, but to exclude, question, and pretty much say anything they want to me or about me" (p. 121). From my perspective, there was an unconscious/unintended expectation by Dan that he could use his discriminatory jokes and colloquialisms as a way of culturally connecting with me. By refusing to accept responsibility for his inappropriate behavior, Dan had constructed a false sense of collegiality with me clouded by his inability or resistance to see his own racist and sexist behavior.

Another way in which issues of legitimation arose for me as a scholar was through the departmental nomination process for university awards. In my third year as an assistant professor, I asked my department administration if my name could be put forth by my undergraduate students for nomination for the University Teacher-Scholar Award. This well-respected award recognizes faculty members who represent the best teachers who have served at the institution for seven years or less, taking into consideration that the most effective teachers have their instruction intricately linked to and informed by their research and creative activities. My undergraduate students asked me if they could put forth my name for consideration, since the nomination instructions indicated that nominations could be put forth by individuals, an administrative unit, or a group. I was told by my department chair that student nomination was not "the typical procedure," and my name was not put forth. Once I had an opportunity to serve on the departmental committee that decides nominations for university awards, I gained an insider perspective on the nomination process. I quickly learned that there was no departmental systematic procedure in place for soliciting names from the broader faculty or for putting forth a particular name. In fact, our committee spent an entire meeting identifying names of faculty members that we thought would be good choices for the university awards, using no clear criteria for committee selections.

In my eighth year as a faculty member, I requested again to have my name put forward for consideration for the award. I was again denied on the basis that I was beyond the time period for nomination, based on university criteria. This was quite disheartening, considering that a White female colleague from my department had been nominated two consecutive years during the time period in which I was eligible. She did not win the award either time. The entire experience underscored a departmental climate issue that rendered Black women and other faculty of color unworthy and unqualified who possessed equivalent or superior qualifications for the warrant of the award. In fact, no faculty member of color had been nominated from our department for the award in at least five years. To be somewhat balanced in my retelling of this story, I should note that my department offered to put forth my name twice for the University Outreach Scholarship Community Partnership Award. This award provides university-wide recognition of highly engaged community-based research collaborations that positively impact both the community and scholarship. I was appreciative of my colleagues' respect for my work with local communities, because the work that faculty of color do in/with their communities of interest is often not rewarded in the academy (Stanley, 2006); nonetheless, the resistance to put forth my name for the Teacher-Scholar Award was an explicit reminder of the lack of recognition that many Black women and other women of color in the academy experience for their research agendas that often relate to their teaching pedagogy and practice (Aguirre, 2000; Thomas & Hollenshead, 2001).

The assaults on my professional and personal identity as described through these two experiences underscore the raced-gendered micro- and macroaggressions that Black female faculty experience in the academy. The double oppressions that we face based on our existence create a dynamic in the workplace where race- and gender-related stress are almost normative. This racial battle fatigue creates a hostile work environment and perpetuates legitimation challenges for the Black female scholar.

83

INCLUSIVE EXCLUSION: THE PERPETUAL OUTSIDER WITHIN

Black female scholars are also perpetual insider-outsiders (Collins, 1991/2008) in PWIs, in part due to our racial minority status rendering us diversity hires, even when our entry into the professional context is not framed as such by our colleagues. On my journey toward tenure at my institution, there were times when I perceived myself as the outsider-within. I was hired in part due to the expertise that I could bring to teacher preparation around topics related to race, culture, and equity, yet I fought for this expertise not to be abused or co-opted in my struggle for inclusion by way of acknowledgment of my ideas for our undergraduate social foundations course and promotion to a leadership position. Furthermore the inclusive exclusion I experienced manifested itself in me having a seat at the table of social justice within my department, yet colleagues' unwillingness to have me sit at the head of the table.

I was one of the few faculty members who taught our social foundations course in the undergraduate teacher preparation program (and the only faculty member of color at the time). This course helped teachers understand how issues of race, class, gender, and other social identity markers impact teaching, learning, and inequity in K-12 schools. In my first year in the department I presented several new readings for the course syllabus to help move the course's framing from being somewhat Eurocentric epistemologically and ideologically. As a result of my input, instructors incorporated my suggestions into their syllabi. In my first three years teaching the course I often aided instructors in understanding how to more critically help future teachers examine race and racism through the course in our weekly instructor team meetings. Dan and others remarked that my voice and background knowledge helped move the course framing and content in a more critically progressive direction.

As Dan began the process of transitioning into retirement, I assumed that I would likely be considered for faculty leadership of the course given the extensive amount of time I had spent mentoring other instructors and improving the content and overall direction of the course. However, a more senior (tenured) White female colleague who had been teaching the course for approximately the same amount of time as me was asked to take leadership of the course. In a private meeting with this colleague I expressed my desire to have a more active role in shaping the vision and direction of the course, and I was told that there were turf issues at play. It became evident to me that prior to my arrival into the department, a few of my White female colleagues had been considered the diversity experts based on their prior teaching experiences in urban contexts and attention to issues of diversity in their scholarship. I perceived that my hiring threatened their positions as the social justice advocates/diversity experts/educational equity warriors.

My identity as a Black woman who makes race and racism in education a central focus of my scholarship, has lived experiences with sexism *and* racism, and has a deep scholarly knowledge base of critical pedagogies, practices, and research pushed against the boundaries of the existing turfs and suggested that someone other than the White (female) social justice scholar could inhabit the "expert space." My array of credentials did not equate to or supersede those that qualified my White female colleagues to maintain sole ownership of the social justice space in our department. I was the outsider-within (Collins, 1991/2008). My voice was valid enough for inclusion of ideas for course planning but not credible enough for vision and leadership planning. Linda Tillman (2012) states of her experience:

> Despite claims of a commitment to diversity, I continue to receive subtle (and sometimes not so subtle) messages that suggest I must never think that my credentials or my contributions to the academy are important. Tolerance, but not acceptance, seems to be the prevailing paradigm.
>
> (p. 121)

I was being tolerated but not accepted. In this way I was inclusively excluded at the social justice table. Patricia Hill Collins (1986) suggests that the outsider-within status is not completely a negative status within the academy. For many Black women, this position provides a certain degree of objectivity that those who are fully immersed in a situation might not be able to have and allows for people to confide in a "stranger" in ways they never would with one another. Framed this way, my outsider-within status might have also posed a threat to my White female colleagues for these reasons, furthering the sense of vulnerability on their part as indicated in my colleague's caution to me about various turfs.

Ultimately after advocating for myself with my department chair, I was able to assume the position of faculty coordinator for the social foundations course; however, this was presented to me as some sort of compromise in that another one of my non-tenure White female colleagues (who also had teaching experience in urban schools) would assume leadership of the urban-focused component of our teacher preparation program. It was as if the message to me was that you can only lead one "diversity" component in our program. I am not sure such negotiations are even discussed in situations where there are no faculty of color with teaching, research, and/or scholarship focus in race/culture/equity areas.

The reader may find that much of what I describe represents an all-too-familiar narrative for Black female professors as well as other women of color in the academy. My hope is that examination of these experiences through raced-gendered lenses can and will move us toward deeper understanding of the need to continue deconstructing the silenced dialogue and hidden curriculum regarding what I call "an epistemology of scholarly identity" in the academy. How we come to understand what it means to be a scholar is defined by neoliberal, colorblind White men. And how female faculty of color (and all faculty, for that matter) come to develop a scholarly identity is embedded within this oppressive construction. Consequently, Black women engage in daily warfare to enact a counter-hegemonic epistemology of scholarly identity, writing and rewriting a counter-narrative of their professional lives that affirms their intellectual and cultural selves. Unfortunately, White men and women consciously and/or subconsciously often become complicit in perpetuating this epistemology to the detriment of the success of Black women and other women of color in the academy. Their behaviors reinforce the regular micro- and macroaggressive assaults on our identities.

I offer three concrete recommendations for non-tenured Black female faculty and other faculty women of color for how to manage and resist raced-gendered micro- and macroaggressions in their journey toward tenure. These strategies helped me immensely along the way.

RECOMMENDATIONS

1. *Establish a community of internal and external mentors.* Identify at least one trustworthy tenured faculty member within your department who can help you learn, navigate, and resist the politics and challenging aspects of the departmental culture. It is also important to establish an advocate at the university level with whom you can share challenges and strategize ways for addressing difficult situations. It is helpful when these mentors are other women of color, but that is not always possible. Having White allies in your community of mentors can also be very valuable to your success on the tenure track.

2. *Do not compromise authenticity for likability.* Be true to who you are. Remember that you were hired for certain personal and professional qualities that your institution deemed as needed and valuable. Engage your work, colleagues, and the institution in ways that allow you to develop and maintain a scholarly identity that remains aligned with your core values and commitments. Being respected for having sound ideological positions and notable scholarship will prove more beneficial than being liked by your colleagues.

3. *Develop a sister circle.* There is a growing body of research on the power of sister circles in higher education for aiding women of color in having positive experiences in academia (as students, faculty, and administrators). Establish a network of Black women and other women of color in your institution. Identify regular times to connect to share experiences and support one another along the journey.

I hope the reader's main take-away from this chapter is not an understanding of my tenure-track experience as one of continual turmoil, trepidation, lack of affirmation, or even inferiority. In fact I had a great deal of support from faculty colleagues along the way. The journey to tenure was one of positive personal and professional self-discovery. I have a heightened awareness of my own tenacity and strength as a "Black-female-scholar"; and while there is a lot of "stuff" that exists between the hyphens in this identity, I am and will continue to be the super-heroine of my destiny and career. The Black female scholar's imposed double jeopardy status is in fact one of our most prized possessions. Out of the ashes we have risen, and we will continue to fight for justice, love, and truth in hopes of tinkering toward an academia that humanizes and normalizes our intelligence and existence as scholars.

REFERENCES

Aguirre, A., Jr. (2000). *Women and minority faculty in the academic workplace: Recruitment, retention, and academic culture*. (ASHE-ERIC Higher Education Rep. No. 27-6.) San Francisco: Jossey-Bass.

Alemán, A. M. (1995). Actuando. In R. Padilla, & R. Chavez (Eds.), *The leaning ivory tower: Latino professors in American universities* (pp. 67–76). Albany, NY: State University of New York Press.

Boyd, T., Cintrón, R., & Alexander-Snow, M. (2010). The experience of being a junior minority faculty member. *The Forum on Public Policy, 2010*(2), 1–23.

Collins, P. H. (1986). Learning from the outsider within: The sociological significance of Black feminist thought. *Social Problems, 33*(6), S14–S32.

Collins, P. H. (1991/2008). *Black feminist thought: Knowledge, consciousness, and the politics of empowerment*. New York, NY: Routledge.

Collins, P. H. (1996). What's in a name? Womanism, Black feminism, and beyond. *Black Scholar, 26*(1), 9–17.

Davis, P. (1989). Law as microaggression. *Yale Law Journal, 98*, 1559–1577.

Gregory, S. T. (2001). Black faculty women in the academy: History, status, and future. *Journal of Negro Education, 70*(3), 124–138.

Harris, T. M. (2007). Black feminist thought and cultural contracts: Understanding the intersection and negotiation of racial, gendered, and professional identities in the academy. *New Directions for Teaching and Learning, 110*, 55–64.

Patton, T. O. (2004). Reflections of a Black woman professor: Racism and sexism in academia. *Harvard Journal of Communication, 15*, 185–200.

Pierce, C., Carew, J., Pierce-Gonzalez, D., & Wills, D. (1978). An experiment in racism: TV commercials. In C. Pierce (Ed.), *Television and education* (pp. 62–88). Beverly Hills, CA: Sage.

Smith, W. A., Yosso, T. J., & Solórzano, D. G. (2006). Challenging racial battle fatigue on historically white campuses: A critical race examination of race-related stress. In C. A. Stanley (Ed.), *Faculty of color: Teaching in predominantly white colleges and universities*. Bolton, MA: Anker Publishing.

Solórzano, D., Ceja, M., & Yosso, T. (2000). Critical race theory, racial microaggressions, and campus racial climate: The experiences of African American college students. *Journal of Negro Education, 69*(1–2), 60–73.

Stanley, C. A. (2006). Coloring the academic landscape: Faculty of color breaking the silence in predominantly white colleges and universities. *American Educational Research Journal, 43*(4), 701–736.

Thomas, G. D., & Hollenshead, C. (2001). Resisting from the margins: The coping strategies of Black women and other women of color faculty members at a research university. *Journal of Negro Education, 70*(3), 166–175.

Tillman, L. C. (2012). Inventing ourselves: an informed essay for Black female scholars in educational leadership. *International Journal of Qualitative Studies in Education, 25*(1), 119–126.

Turner, C., & Meyers, S. Jr. (2000). *Faculty of color in academe: Bittersweet success.* Boston: Allyn & Bacon.

Chapter 9

Black Queer (Re)presentation in (White) Academe

I am the Hell and the High Water

Dafina-Lazarus Stewart

The stereotyped tropes of Black womanhood that have pervaded U.S. society over the past 400 years generally present Black women as either asexual or hypersexual, but always as non-feminine (Collins, 1990/2008). Black women have long been held outside the confines of true womanhood, rendering them vulnerable to countless methods of victimization (hooks, 1990). Nonetheless, this outsider status also has been used by Black women to defy European standards of beauty and build counter-narratives of Black womanhood that celebrate the physical features and behavioral traits that have been denigrated by a dominant White society (Collins, 1986, 1990/2008). Although Mammy, Sapphire, and Jezebel stereotypes misrepresent authentic Black women (Collins, 1986; West, 1995; White, 2007), they share something with the Black women counter-narratives that seek to self-define and self-evaluate Black women's lives (Collins, 1986). Both these external stereotypes and internal narratives told by Black sororities, Black church matrons, and Afrocentric femininity all ignore and render invisible Black queer women.

Black queer women's transgressive sexuality has been portrayed in fictional accounts, like Gloria Naylor's (1983) *The Women of Brewster Place*, as closeted, mysterious, and often a threat to Black masculinity. As dangerous and threatening, Black queer women have been subjected to physical violence, as well as assaults both sexual (corrective rape) and verbal (pejoratives such as "bulldaggers"). Despite maintaining critical roles in the Black community, the status and experiences of Black queer women are marginalized in discussions about Black community welfare (Moore, 2011). In the academy, where Blackness lacks intersections with gender and sexuality, Black queer women occupy an invisible, outsider status in predominantly White faculty spaces as well as in predominantly heterosexual Black faculty spaces. Black queer women's (re)presentations challenge socialization norms and the mores of faculty culture through their engagement with body politics, stereotypical tropes, and hyper-/invisibility. Predominantly White institutions, like the rest of society, have not adopted an intersectional approach to the integration of racially minoritized faculty, staff, or students. Consequently, Black queer women, collapsed with Black men (gay and straight) and Black heterosexual women, have been presented only as Black, ignoring or diminishing their distinctive sexuality and gender identities.

Audre Lorde (1984) once reflected that she was constantly asked to "pluck out some one aspect of herself and present that as the meaningful whole" (p. 120). Lorde refused to do so, saying that her "fullest concentration of energy" (p. 120) was only available to her when she integrated the various aspects of herself, allowing the power from each aspect to flow to and through each other in the service of the struggles which she embraced. Likewise, I made a decision in 2008 to throw off the external definitions of Black womanhood that I had adopted and to begin to (re)present an authentic self that defied conventional wisdom about how I would "show up" as raced, gendered, and sexed in the academy. My experiences navigating institutional climates before and after 2008 highlight the ways in which gender and sexuality are racialized in predominantly White institutions.

I use Black feminist thought (Collins 1986, 1990/2008) and elements of critical race theory ([CRT] Delgado & Stefancic, 2012; Ladson-Billings, 1998) to examine the intersection of race, sexuality, and gender identity and expression in my experiences as a Black queer faculty member. Work by Phelan (1993) and Butler (1991), as well as Young's (1990) analysis of social groups, are brought alongside Black feminist thought and CRT to speak to the ways that both race and gender identities are performed in public spheres and used to create insiders and outsiders within and across the multiple and overlapping social groups that Black queer women navigate in the academy. Scholarly personal narrative (Nash & Viray, 2013) is the method employed to deeply analyze the ways that Black and queer (re)presentations in the academy bring "hell and high water" on body politics, stereotypic tropes, and hyper-/invisibility. Through this analysis, a counter-narrative will emerge that disrupts the additive, unitary approach to current discussions of faculty diversity and, in particular, the experiences of Black faculty in predominantly White institutions.

HELL AND HIGH WATER: COMING OUT IN ACADEME

I did not begin my faculty career as an out lesbian. In fact, I would describe myself as the exact opposite: I was divorced with a daughter and practicing serial monogamy. After several years of cutting my hair and then growing it back, when I took my first tenure-track faculty position in 2002 at the age of 28, I had long, heavy, thick black hair that was chemically straightened (i.e., "relaxed"). As another Black woman colleague would describe me, I was a "Barbie doll dipped in chocolate." It was a description I was not at all comfortable with as it felt awfully close to being called an "oreo" despite the fact that my friend and colleague did not mean that at all. My unease had far more to do with me, though; a fact that would eventually become glaringly apparent. But until then, I did my best to act the role I thought I was supposed to play.

Since I was so much younger than my faculty colleagues (the next youngest person at my first institution was at least 12 years my senior; at my next institution the next youngest was 10 years my senior) and so close in age to my graduate-level students, I went out of my way to dress professionally and to look older. I deliberately chose outfits that were well-fitting and stylish, but in that style most appropriate for a woman approaching 50, not one approaching 30. I modeled long skirts that swept my ankles, structured jackets, and bulky sweaters in the winter. I wore light cosmetics even though I hated it and heels as often as possible. My expression was stern, revealing little of what lay behind my eyes, and I was cautious not to share any of my personal life with either colleagues or students. I continued on like this for my first six years in the academy as a tenure-track assistant professor, feeling more and more trapped with each passing year while battling depression and an undiagnosed attention-deficit disorder.

But then, in July 2008, the hell and the high water came in the form of my coming out—first to myself and then gradually to others—that I was gay. It was truly a catharsis, a watershed moment; authenticity washing over me like a mighty stream. But here I was, a year from submitting my promotion and tenure portfolio and uncertain of how my "news" would be received. I figured my department colleagues would be very supportive and they were. I was not the only non-heterosexual person on the faculty and these were student affairs faculty after all, known as a group to be open and affirming. No, it was not my departmental colleagues who I worried about. When I came out, I was keenly aware that there were no other—not a single—queer person of color still at the university as faculty or staff. There had been two or three in the past, but they were long gone by the time I came out and began looking for community. My concerns centered on the apparently exclusively heterosexual Black faculty and staff population at my institution and the fact that I lived in a predominantly White, rural town with no evident community of queer people of color (QPOC) anywhere in sight. Long aware of the racism in White queer communities, I also wondered if I would feel comfortable in predominantly White queer spaces. Would I find myself ostracized from my Black colleagues when they found out that I was gay? Was I destined (or doomed) to be the only QPOC faculty or staff person on campus? The questions swirled in my mind with the intensity of a tropical storm.

Meanwhile, I quickly made up lost time and peeled back all those trappings of Black feminist respectability (White, 2001) that had kept me closeted for so long. In so doing, I discovered that answering my questions would reveal paradoxes that would illustrate that I had not unleashed hell or high water with my Black queer (re)presentation; rather, my Black queer (re)presentation was

91

needed to *withstand* both the hell and the high water that had been ready to breach the dam all along.

BODY POLITICS AND FETISHIZING THE QUEER

The more comfortable I became with my truth, the more I let go of the costumes I had used to perform a heterosexual feminine identity. Although there is no standardized identity performance (Phelan, 1993), mine had been carefully constructed to be recognizable as a *Black heterosexual woman* (i.e., feminine). The architects of this construction were a mother who put herself through finishing school; an all-girls, predominantly White high school; and the raced and gendered cultural styles of the bourgeois Black church. My "Academy Award-winning performance," as one student remarked in reaction to my coming out to him, was gradually but deliberately dropped. The ankle-sweeping skirts and bulky sweaters, already replaced by more youthful-looking knee-length career skirts and blazers, were themselves supplanted by men's dress slacks and shirts, ties, sport coats, and men's shoes, and later bowties and three-piece suits.

As my gender presentation became decidedly more masculine—making my queer sexuality more apparent to those who believed that all lesbians dressed like men—the reactions from various campus constituencies varied from bemused delight to fascination to obsession. For the QPOC undergraduate student population, my more obvious queer identity was a cause for celebration and attracted a level of attention I had not anticipated. Among the graduate students in my department, White gay men seemed to be particularly fascinated by this Black female body moving lithely about in men's clothing with so much freedom. I was called a "dandy." I had never thought of myself in that way before and was not sure that it really fit me. True, I was a stylish dresser, but I had always been—even in my middle-aged attire.

Other Black faculty and staff seemed either confused or deliberately ignored that any change had taken place at all. One morning while waiting for the elevator in my building, a fellow Black female administrator noticed my tie and asked, "So what is that about?" Students of color in my department were either uncertain and cautious or welcoming depending on their own level of comfort with queer people or self-identified queerness. This was a significant departure from establishing the easy rapport to which I had become accustomed. When I went to professional conferences, although I was not the only Black female with a transmasculine performance, I was the only Black female *faculty* member exhibiting one. As a close friend, who is a gay Black man, explains to me on a regular basis with sparkles in his eyes, "They just don't know *what* to do with you."

There is a word for things that are both fascinating and puzzling—*exotic*. I had become exotic. And with my newfound exoticism came a level of "unquestioning reverence [and] devotion," *fetish* (Dictionary.com, 2013), which I had never experienced before——nor which I had ever witnessed to be showered upon any Black [heterosexual] woman faculty I had known. The literature clearly portrays Black and other women of color faculty as besieged in their own classes by racial microaggressions, tormented by disrespect and dismissal at the hands of racially privileged and entitled White students and some students of color with a sense of entitlement rooted in faux racial solidarity (Butner, Burley, & Marbley, 2000; Constantine, Smith, Redington, & Owens, 2008; McGowan, 2000; Patton & Catching, 2009; Stanley, Porter, Simpson, & Ouellett, 2003; Vargas, 2002). Although I have had to deal with students who challenged my expertise and were disrespectful of my status, those instances had become so rare as to be almost non-existent (whereas before I came out and altered my dress they were as persistent as they are reflected to be in the literature). When some (usually) new student would try to exert (usually) his privilege, they were often corrected by other students in the class before I could come to my own defense. My daily experiences were characterized by students filling my class sections within the first five minutes of open registration; asking to have me as their advisor; genuinely feeling cheated by my sabbatical year which had deprived them of an opportunity to take a class with me; and eager upon my return from sabbatical to learn what classes I would be teaching the coming year. I began to enjoy a level of popularity and unqualified respect that I had never known in my career. Students, undergraduate and graduate, were seemingly in love with me before they even met me. I was truly mystified and deeply concerned as I listened to other Black faculty colleagues whose experiences were radically different and markedly more negative than my own. Was I not providing sufficient challenge? Had I left heteronormativity and White privilege unquestioned and become *too* comfortable to be around? What else could explain such fetishistic behavior usually reserved for Black people regarded as "[Uncle] Toms" and panderers to White patriarchy as I had witnessed it all my life? It would seem that I had become the ultimate queer "magic Negro" (Baldwin, 2003).

STEREOTYPIC TROPES AND THE OUTSIDER-WITHIN

Despite being a fetishized object, I still encountered contradictory expectations for my role and the nature of my interpersonal interactions with others. On one hand, I was presumed to be no-nonsense, prone to exhibit anger at the drop of a hat, and generally to embody all the characteristics of a military drill sergeant. A colleague told me that she perceived me to react often above and beyond (what she thought) the situation called for. When a student would fall short of expectations, warnings would be delivered on my behalf, reminiscent of a child's sing-song half-gleeful taunt: "Ooo, you're in trouble now!" Someone who had never had me as an instructor warned one of my students not to expect me to be "soft" on him if he ran into challenges fulfilling the course requirements. I was frequently told

93

by students that I was "intimidating" and "stern"—unless *I* relaxed. Apparently, I was prone to become a black-skinned Mr. Hyde at any moment. Reminiscent of the emasculating Jezebel (West, 1995; White, 2007), I united both the "angry Black woman" and "angry lesbian" in my Black transmasculine body. Threatening and dangerous, I needed to be approached with caution. I managed this feat without expending any effort, while other (White) faculty would largely escape such characterizations despite displaying similar attitudes, behaviors, and reactions just as much, if not more frequently.

Yet, I was not only an emasculating Jezebel. Because so many students were enamored with me, I was also heralded as nurturing, compassionate, and the person to turn to if you needed to be rescued. Yet, I witnessed others dismiss my needs as legitimate and render my presence unimportant when it came to community engagement. My expressions of dissatisfaction and disagreement were met at times with mystified surprise. My recommendations and suggestions were treated as intrusions unless they were specifically invited. Those invitations mostly came regarding relational and group dynamics and student issues, *not* my research and scholarship. I was both Jezebel and Mammy (West, 1995; White, 2007). Images of the Black Mammy have long pervaded literature and popular culture (West, 1995), often as domestic workers employed by economically privileged White families, who cooked, cleaned, and raised legions of White children who would grow up to both adore and treat her like so much chattel. Most recently, a quintessential Mammy portrait was drawn in Kathryn Stockett's novel (2009) *The Help*, and powerfully brought to life by Viola Davis' Oscar-nominated performance in the film. It became clear to me that I was functioning as a Mammy for my department. As the granddaughter of a domestic, I am struck by the intractability of this role despite the wide gulf in professional and social class status that separates my Grandma Lucille and me.

The dark irony of the Mammy figure is the juxtaposition of dependence and disposal. On the one hand, the family she works for espouses her virtues, threatens self-harm were she to depart, and promises to take care of her. The Mammy appears to be warmly accepted as a valued member of the family. Yet, on the other hand, this "family" often fails to include her as an equal in family activities or includes her only in her role as handmaiden to the family's needs. She knows she can never truly be a member of the family despite the mutual benefits which accrue due to her insider position within the family structure (Collins, 1986). She is ultimately only valuable and valued so long as she stays in her place, attends to the family, and silences her own life and needs, rendering them invisible. Moreover, at least superficially, she may collude with the family's incomplete interpretations and evaluations of who she is (Collins, 1986). Collins (1986) identified Black female domestics, like my Grandma Lucille, as "outsider[s]-within." Though separated from my grandmother's experiences by several decades and two generations of genealogical progress gained via educational attainment, I nevertheless find myself to be a Black domestic worker in the academy, one of Collins' outsiders-within.

As later clarified by Collins (1999), the *outsider-within* "describes social locations or border spaces occupied by groups of unequal power [and individuals who are members of those groups]" (p. 86) within dominant structures. Individuals from marginalized groups can use their outsider-within location as a kind of corrective lens that brings the organization into sharper focus, more clearly magnifying the organization's gaps and blind spots regarding justice and inclusion (Collins, 1986, 1999). Deeply rooted in an intersectional perspective, Collins' outsider-within construct asserted that those located within multiple axes of marginality (race x sex x social class x sexuality x gender), thus affected by several systems of domination, "will develop a sharper view of the interlocking nature of oppression" (Collins, 1986, p. S19, footnote 10; Lorde, 1984).

In addition to the characteristics discussed above, also central to the Mammy trope is the belief that the Mammy has limited knowledge and skills and what she does possess is meant solely for the benefit of her employing family. I am a person who holds multiple oppressed identities within race, sex, gender, sexuality, and ability and have continually expanded my scholarship to include multiple areas of diversity and systems of oppression and a breadth of methodological skills. Although I have been easily afforded validity as a diversity expert—a backhanded benefit of the sharper focus gained through years of functioning within the academy as an outsider-within—that expertise is continually restricted only to issues of race. In a department meeting, I was once explicitly challenged about my ability to teach aspects of diversity other than race. I also have to overcompensate for students' inability to see beyond my race and the assumption that I can only talk about race by being hyper-vigilant in using illustrations from a variety of social groups and oppressive systems. The relevance and significance of my queer sexuality and transgressive gender is erased, nullified, and subordinated in the service of my more valuable racial identity as a commodity of whiteness.

Despite this, for several semesters, my sections of the department's multicultural competence course would quickly reach maximum enrollment while other students begged to be granted entrance. Yet, other sections taught by a White colleague with a different mix of marginalized identities and equivalent social justice expertise struggled to meet minimum enrollment expectations. Once I was told by some students of color that although they were waiting to take my multicultural competence section, they had elected to take another core course from a White male faculty member they deemed to be a more reliable expert in that subject. Students and other faculty have referred in singular terms to faculty expertise in issues not related to race within the department, ignoring my broader and more recent publication, presentation, and professional service record in those same areas. That I would have interests, talents, and skills outside those which directly related to my race and therefore were most valuable to the department was met with suspicion and disregard.

VISIBLY INVISIBLE

The hyper-visibility of my racial identity parallels the experiences of other Black faculty in predominantly White institutions (Patton & Catching, 2009). However, this racial hyper-visibility does not bring my other social group memberships into sharper focus for those around me. Instead, my queerness, as performed by my sexuality and gender identity and expression, is pushed to the margins of my identity. When I came out and rumors of my queer sexuality began to spread through the Black faculty and staff community, I was no longer specially invited to attend campus race-focused functions and my posts to the community's listserv often went unacknowledged. Since I did not come to my institution as an out gay person, I can note the stark difference between how Black faculty and staff communities engaged me during my first years as a faculty member and how I have been regarded since I came out. As my queer identities became more pronounced, slowly, but deliberately, I became invisible to the Black faculty and staff community. My perceived "gender insubordination" (Butler, 1991) did not fit with the cultural mores that shaped and informed Black faculty and staff culture—the norms which tacitly drew the lines of social group identity (Young, 1990), in this case, authentic Blackness (Harris & Khanna, 2010), in ways that excluded queer representations. My queer performances (Phelan, 1993), performed most clearly in my chosen "costume" of men's attire and masculine haircut, seemed to have rendered me non-Black, an adaptation of Wittig's (1992) construction of the lesbian as "non-woman."

This same erasure of my queer gender identity takes place occasionally in other spaces, as well. Despite the fact that I customarily only wear men's clothing and accessories, I routinely encounter people who overlook that fact. Recently, at the conclusion of an impromptu meeting with me, a White male student in my department complimented the clearly masculine sport coat I was wearing and further commented, "See, women's clothes are so much cooler. You have so many more options." When I informed him that the item was actually purchased in the men's department, the student seemed genuinely confused and muttered a farewell and awkwardly left my office. Perhaps my gender expression did not align with the performance of Blackness with which this White student was familiar. Or, my racial alterity was so overwhelming that all other identities receded to the background. In either case, the hyper-visibility of my racial presence in the minds of others seemed both to obfuscate and marginalize other relevant aspects of my personhood.

Invisibility also informed my experience in other ways, affecting my whole being. From being overlooked by a senior colleague when the conversation turned to identifying "talented" and "up and coming" scholars for faculty recruitment to persistent accusations that I am unavailable despite being on campus for 40 or more hours each week, the whole of my being is cloistered and pushed out of the room. I do not exist until I am sought. If I am sought and not found then I am always absent. My uninvited presence—whole, complete, and authentic—reflects the typical resistance of dominant systems to fully engage the "serious consequences of [B]lacks" (Morrison, 1992, p. 67). As Collins (1999) speculated, diverse bodies without inclusive structures "substitutes for substantive, organizational change" (p. 88) failing to "*eliminate* outsider-within locations . . . by including Black women in new ways" (p. 88, emphasis in original). In the absence of transformative organizational change, it does not matter who is brought in to diversify the look of the "family" as long as whoever is chosen "convincingly play[s] the part" (Collins, 1999, p. 88). And so we come full circle. Am I fated to be Baldwin's (2003) queered magic Negro?

(RE)PRESENTATION

The compounded microaggressions I encounter as a Black female queer faculty member reflect the interlocking nature of oppression emphasized by Black feminist thought (Collins, 1986, 1990/2008) and CRT scholarship (Delgado & Stefancic, 2012; Ladson-Billings, 1998). Although commonalities exist between my experiences and other Black faculty irrespective of sex, gender, and sexuality (Patton & Catching, 2009), the added marginality of my sexuality and gender expression serve to further refine the standpoint I bring to conversations about social justice in the academy (Collins, 1986). As an outsider-within among both the predominantly White macrocosm and the predominantly heteronormative Black microcosm, I am afforded a unique location in the academy.

Identity performances are located in contested spaces. Authentic representations of one's social group memberships (Young, 1990) are complicated when no single, unitary social group membership is central to one's identity performance. When heteronormative Blackness is the only externally validated identity performance afforded to Black queer faculty, multiple axes of marginality can be used to "flip the script" and move the margins to the center and the center to the margins (hooks, 2000). As can happen with drag performances which distort femininity and masculinity, the subjectification (through a process of claiming and internalizing what has been projected as unattainable) of what has been centered and privileged opens up useful debate about the meaning and relevance of what is authentic and what is reflection. In like manner, the performances of Black queer faculty that emerge from their sexuality and gender deconstruct and (re)present Blackness to allow that which is regarded as faithful to be examined, critiqued, and transformed.

Toward that end, as Collins (1986) has articulated, the domestic and her employing family share mutual satisfaction and on some level she must cooperate with the family's incomplete representations and evaluations of her. Indeed, toothy smiles and sly grins often betray my willing cooperation with both my Mammy and Jezebel performances. Being the receptor of inside information and seen as a valuable resource for support and problem-solving does feel affirming in many ways, and I cannot deny my mischievous delight in the knowledge of my intimidating persona.

Collusion, however, is not the whole story. The outsider-within also engages in continual self-definition and self-evaluation necessary to maintain an internal compass capable of charting one's own identity (Collins, 1986). Messages of insufficiency, limited utility, and invisibility are countered with self-definitions and self-evaluations that affirm my holistic worth, value, and the transformative power of my presence. Instead of exhausting myself by constantly working in my office with my door open for persistent interruption, I honor my own needs for effective work conditions and exhort myself to adhere to them, while communicating those needs to others. Whether requested or not, I consistently speak up for equity and justice, making myself visible where others would prefer I be invisible, and present where some would prefer my absence.

Finally, my experiences demonstrate the necessity of redefining community in opposition to norms for engagement which rest on salient single, unitary social group memberships. As Moya (2009) suggests for the classroom, developing communities of meaning in the academy for Black queer faculty can also lead to the elimination of the outsider-within status exhorted by Collins (1999). Communities of meaning mobilize the epistemic significance of identities to create across, within, and between bridges of understanding, communication, and activism (Moya, 2009). They can help to dismantle oppressively narrow identity subjectivities by engaging the convergence of multiple identities and the interlocking nature of oppression.

Fortunately, since I came out, there are now a half-dozen queer people of color who are faculty or staff, and their presence has made my own less invisible. I have not allowed others to dictate what spaces I enter or exit, surrendering to social isolation. Rather, I continue to be present within Black faculty and staff spaces, as well as within predominantly White spaces, in all my Blackness, queer sexuality, and gender non-conforming authenticity. By practicing intentional critique of exclusive practices, I have witnessed the slow process of transformation begin to take shape. Although threatened and fearful that my coming out would unleash an unmanageable personal and professional complexity, this has not come to pass. Instead, by embracing my power as a force of nature to catalyze others and my surroundings, I have claimed an intersectional standpoint perspective that can lead to transgressive action and transformation: I am the hell and the high water.

98

RECOMMENDATIONS

What I have learned from my experiences in the academy as a Black queer faculty member suggests the following for others who may find themselves similarly situated:

- *Define yourself for yourself.* Despite how others may be tempted to define you, protect your sense of self by being clear on who you are, what you value, and why you do the work that you do.

- *Resist internalizing either compliments or criticisms.* There will be some who think you are the most phenomenal teacher they have ever had and others who think your scholarship is trivial. Neither of those opinions should substantively affect your self-concept.

- *Be intentional about building and maintaining a supportive network of colleagues.* You may need to build this network beyond your institution, but having people to talk to, to process situations with, and to give and receive encouragement is fundamental to thriving in the academy.

- *Make that support network polyvocal and multifaceted.* As I mentioned above, those who exist at the intersections of multiple marginalizations are ill-served by communities defined by single, unitary components of identity. Developing the ability to move between and among various social worlds will limit isolation and hone your perceptual acuity.

- *Cultivate people to be allies.* Allyship is a skill that requires practice and practice needs to be corrected and coached. Although it can become wearisome, you must teach people how to treat you.

- *Keep growing, becoming, evolving.* Whatever has brought you to this point, your journey is not over. Do not allow your current performance of self to become the box that limits your continued growth and evolution. Others, who watch from the sidelines, may not understand but they will come to value your willingness to continue evolving.

- *Be authentic.* This is a recommendation given elsewhere in this volume and it deserves to be repeated. Your authenticity is important for your own self-care, but it also allows others to be authentic. We are not here for ourselves, but as a light and witness to others. As an anonymous person once said, "You have to be brave with your life, so that others can be brave with theirs."

REFERENCES

Baldwin, G. (2003). What a difference a gay makes: Queering the magic Negro. *Journal of Religion and Popular Culture, 5*(1), 3–13.

Butler, J. (1991). Imitation and gender insubordination. In D. Fuss (Ed.), *Inside/out: Lesbian theories, gay theories* (pp. 13–31). New York, NY: Routledge.

99

Butner, B. K., Burley, H., & Marbley, A. F. (2000). Coping with the unexpected: Black faculty at predominantly White institutions. *Journal of Black Studies, 30*(3), 453–462.

Collins, P. H. (1986). Learning from the outsider within: The sociological significance of Black feminist thought. *Social Problems, 33*(6), S14–S32.

Collins, P. H. (1990/2008). *Black feminist thought: Knowledge, consciousness, and the politics of empowerment.* New York, NY: Routledge.

Collins, P. H. (1999). Reflections on the outsider within. *Journal of Career Development, 26*(1), 85–88.

Constantine, M. G., Smith, L., Redington, R. M., & Owens, D. (2008). Racial microaggressions against Black counseling and counseling psychology faculty: A central challenge in the multicultural counseling movement. *Journal of Counseling and Development, 86*(3), 348–355.

Delgado, R., & Stefancic, J. (2012). *Critical race theory: An introduction* (2nd ed.). New York, NY: New York University.

Dictionary.com. (2013, October 11). Fetish. Retrieved October 11, 2013 from: http://dictionary.reference.com/browse/fetish?s=t&ld=1171.

Harris, C. A., & Khanna, N. (2010). Black is, Black ain't: Biracials, middle-class Blacks, and the social construction of Blackness. *Sociological Spectrum: Mid-South Sociological Association, 30*(6), 639–670.

hooks, b. (1990). *Yearning: Race, gender, and cultural politics.* Cambridge, MA: South End Press.

hooks, b. (2000). *Feminist theory: From margin to center.* Cambridge, MA: South End Press.

Ladson-Billings, G. (1998). Just what is critical race theory and what's it doing in a nice field like education? *Qualitative Studies in Education, 11*(1), 7–24.

Lorde, A. (1984). *Sister outsider: Essays and speeches by Audre Lorde.* Freedom, CA: Crossing Press.

McGowan, J. M. (2000). African-American faculty classroom teaching experiences in predominantly White colleges and universities. *Multicultural Education, 8*(2), 19–22.

Moore, M. (2011). *Invisible families: Gay identities, relationships, and motherhood among Black women.* Berkeley, CA: University of California Press.

Morrison, T. (1992). *Playing in the dark: Whiteness and the literary imagination.* Cambridge, MA: Harvard University Press.

Moya, P. M. L. (2009). What's identity got to do with it? Mobilizing identities in the multicultural classroom. In S. Sánchez-Casal & A. A. Macdonald (Eds.), *Identity in education* (pp. 45–64). New York, NY: Palgrave Macmillan.

Nash, R. J., & Viray, S. (2013). *Our stories matter: Liberating the voices of marginalized students through scholarly personal narrative writing.* New York, NY: Peter Lang.

Naylor, G. (1983). *The women of Brewster Place.* New York, NY: Penguin Books.

Patton, L. D., & Catching, C. (2009). "Teaching while Black": Narratives of African American student affairs faculty. *International Journal of Qualitative Studies in Education, 22*(6), 713–728.

Phelan, P. (1993). *Unmarked: The politics of performance*. New York, NY: Routledge.

Stanley, C. A., Porter, M. E., Simpson, M., & Ouellett, M. E. (2003). A case study of the teaching experiences of African American faculty at two predominantly White research universities. *Journal on Excellence in College Teaching, 14*(1), 151–178.

Stockett, K. (2009). *The help*. New York, NY: Penguin.

Vargas, L. (Ed.). (2002). *Women faculty of color in the White classroom*. New York, NY: Peter Lang.

West, C. M. (1995). Mammy, Sapphire, and Jezebel: Historical images of Black women and their implications for psychotherapy. *Psychotherapy: Theory, Research, Practice, Training, 32*(3), 458–466.

White, D. G. (2007). Jezebel and Mammy: The mythology of female slavery. In J. F. Healy, & E. O'Brien (Eds.), *Race, ethnicity, and gender: Selected readings* (2nd ed., pp. 124–132). Thousand Oaks, CA: Pine Forge Press.

White, E. F. (2001). *Dark continents of our bodies: Black feminism and the politics of respectability*. Philadelphia, PA: Temple University Press.

Wittig, M. (1992). *"The straight mind" and other essays*. Boston, MA: Beacon Press.

Young, I. M. (1990). Five faces of oppression. In I. M. Young (Ed.), *Justice and the politics of difference* (pp. 39–65). Princeton, NJ: Princeton University Press.

Part III

Black Faculty

Finding Strength through Critical
Mentoring Relationships

Self-Reflection as a Critical Tool in the Life of an Early Career African American Male Scholar

Alonzo M. Flowers III

Prior to writing this book chapter, I did not have significant amount of time allocated to evaluate the faculty experience, particularly from the viewpoint of an assistant professor who happens to be the only African American male within the entire College of Education. Therefore, this book chapter proved to be a therapeutic outlet for me as I contemplated my experiences within my university. Still it is important to note that the inclination and struggle of new assistant professors are not only riddled with career-related stressors (e.g., research, publications, teaching) but rather also find themselves in a transitional space for self. Hagedorn (2000), for instance, posits that faculty from racial and ethnic backgrounds are disproportionately impacted by stressors that affect job satisfaction and longevity of employment. Such stressors can often be problematic as faculty try to professionally and socially acclimate to the environment, both on and off campus. Based on my experiences, these issues of professional and social acclimation became painfully real in my first two years as an assistant professor.

This chapter provides a Scholarly Personal Narrative of my authentic experiences of my first two years in the academy as an assistant professor at a research-intensive university. More specifically, the first half of this chapter showcases my thoughts and experiences in my first two years as an assistant professor that resulted from extensive critical dialogue exchanges with a colleague. The latter half of the chapter conceptualizes my experiences within the realm of the literature that focuses on the experiences of faculty of color in the academy.

As previously mentioned, the academy moves so quickly that there is no time for self-reflection. While annual departmental evaluations prompt reflection in a mechanical manner, candid conversations with a long-time friend and colleague, Rosie M. Banda, a Latina Ph.D. herself who is uncertain about whether or not to enter the academy, sparked raw and unrestricted dialogue about what truly happens within the academy. This narrative inquiry provides a frame of discussion based on the premise that as individuals we come to understand our experiences and give them meaning through the narration of story (Andrews, Squire, & Tambokou, 2008). Josselson (2006) similarly notes that the complexity of human lived experiences provides insight to the constructed lives that individuals live. Based on my experiences this is the central construction of how I have come to reflect on my past two years in the academy. Even though I recognize that two years in the academy is a drop in the bucket compared to seasoned faculty members, it is my belief that these two years have unhinged experiences that are comparative to the literature on faculty of color that I once read while in my graduate courses. Unable to discuss these experiences freely with my colleagues, I sought out a former classmate, long-time friend, fellow colleague, and scholar to engage in critical discussions about some of the problematic elements of being an African American assistant professor at a predominantly White institution (PWI). What follows is one of our candid dialogues on one winter day during the second year of my employment at my institution.

CANDID DIALOGUES

Most of my true reflection of my experiences in my first two years as an assistant professor started as a result of a simple question such as "How's it going in your new position?" To most, the question is straightforward. Short. Sweet. And, to the point. But, the response to this simple question proved to be more complex than I ever even imagined. Where do I start? What aspect do you want to know about? I often rambled, fumbled, and griped through the responses before I could fully and coherently articulate what I truly experienced on any given day. Most of my responses could be categorized in two ways: professional and personal.

Professionally, I shared that I enjoyed my colleagues and the mission and direction of the institution. I also recognized that there were several mechanisms of support; however, I often felt that the support was superficially driven. For instance, the institution provided a substantial research package to help assist the development of my research agenda. Yet, there were few senior faculty members within my department who I could collaborate with on research projects examining issues of men of color and academic transitional issues. It seemed that my primary research focus on African American and Latino males left me isolated from a majority of my colleagues, who predominantly focused their research on higher education issues outside the scope of diversity. This is not to say that research areas outside of my focus lack merit, but my need to engage in critical discussions about similar research interests left me absent and mute from the opportunity to intellectually engage in dialogue with my colleagues. I, as a result, sought dialogue and strengthened professional relationships with colleagues outside of both my college and university. The void that I felt was, in other words, filled by colleagues, who were often hundreds or thousands of miles away. I struggled with this type of intellectual isolation. Ambrose, Huston, and Norman (2005) indicate that critical support in collegiality is integral for continuous development and support for tenure-track faculty members. Consequently, African American male faculty members often find it difficult to create scholarly alliances that perpetuate and reinforce their research agendas typically focusing on issues of diversity (Flowers & Jones, 2003; Jackson, 2003).

On this given day when Banda asked me "How's it going?" I am certain she thought she would receive a simple "It's good. Great." Or, "It's going okay" rather than an explication that lasted well over 30 minutes that addressed an issue that was far more complex than I could even articulate. These types of conversations became a norm, as Banda served as my sounding board to not only vent my frustrations but also to make meaning of my experiences in a deeper and more reflective manner. We both quickly learned that simple, straightforward questions no longer would have simple, straightforward responses within the context of my experiences within the academy. Our candid conversations over the last few years were not only limited to the professional aspect of my experiences in the academy, but also challenged me to confront the social acclimation and my space in my sense of self as I relocated my life to another state.

Addressing the professional aspect of my experiences, while difficult and challenging at times, proved easier to understand and grapple mainly because the scholar in me naturally resorted to literature to make sense of what I was experiencing. I knew from being steeped in the research that my feelings of professional isolation were not only my struggle, and my training at my doctoral institution socialized me to expect the professional challenges that I have encountered and continue to encounter. However, what remains absent from the literature and from most conversations with senior colleagues is a critical dialogue that highlights the struggles that one encounters when they relocate their life to another state. Oftentimes, I believe, the focus remains on faculty acclimation to the institution and expectations as a junior faculty member with little to minimal discussion about the holistic experience of assistant professors. Tinto's (1997) work, for instance, highlights the importance of social and academic integration for students in order to persist at institutions of higher education. Can the same not be said for faculty members?

For the few who know me outside of the academy, I have a fiercely small but closely knitted group of friends who I embrace as my second family. In my relocation to my new institution, I assumed that there would be an abundance of young professionals I could potentially befriend and establish new social and professional networks. However, I found this process to be problematic due to the fact that a majority of the faculty within my department and on campus were older and often had family responsibilities. To put in context, when I left my home state I moved to another state approximately 1,600 miles away from my spouse, my dogs, my family, and my friends. This practice of living bi-coastal is a

107

commonly accepted and almost predictable way of life for many young scholars entering the academy. While there is ample research that focuses on the experiences of faculty of color in the academy (see Antonio, 2002; Defleur, 2007; Diggs, Garrison-Wade, Estrada, & Galindo, 2009; Moore, 2000; Stanley, 2006), little research exists that substantiates faculty experiences as they transition socially into their academic environments, as both a professional and a member of a new community.

My personal experiences have been the most difficult for me to grapple within the transitional process that encapsulates both a professional and personal aspect. Within the scope of developing new relationships, I failed to find significant connections with individuals on campus. Outside a professional sense, I sought a work–life balance to ensure my growth holistically not only as a faculty member but as an individual as well. I quickly realized that my institution did not adequately provide social support in the form of outside organizations and networks for young faculty members. While I was able to develop some relationships via outside a structured university support, I still felt socially isolated. For instance, my first Thanksgiving I received no formal invitations to spend the holiday with colleagues or friends who lived in the area. Rather, I spent Thanksgiving alone. By myself. I prepared a Thanksgiving feast for several, even though I was the only one to attend. To be certain, I could have traveled home for the holiday but it made no financial and travel sense to fly home for a week only to return home a week later. This particular Thanksgiving—my favorite holiday due to my self-induced food coma—was a sobering and ugly reality of how I had socially isolated myself. More importantly, it painted a poignant picture of something that I never wanted to experience again. This was the first time that I embraced and decided that I needed to relocate myself to another institution that was closer to home so that I could be within driving distance of family and friends.

While I initially only considered my need to fit into the academic and professional aspects as an assistant professor, the experience of spending my first Thanksgiving alone prompted me to critically reflect on the importance of social fit within my environment. So, the simple, straightforward question of "How's it going?" had responses that transcended the professional aspect of my daily interactions but just as important focused on how I was fitting in socially. The lack of research on this aspect of social acclimation for faculty members left me at a loss when I attempted to find a theoretical understanding of my experience. My need and search to substantiate *every* aspect of my life with research left me with many unanswered questions as I struggled to acclimate socially in my new environment. Consequently, my discussions with Banda led me to re-evaluate particular value structures (e.g., family, friends, and work–life balance) that were not previously a conscious part of my periphery. With a sounding board in Banda and discussions with other colleagues who made the transitional move to pursue a faculty appointment out of state, I realized that there is a dire and critical need for faculty to establish and nurture professional and social networks. Such a sentiment is supported by Antonio (2003), who highlights the critical need for a comprehensively supportive institutional environment for faculty of color. Throughout the many dialogues with Banda, I have been able to reflect and conceptualize three critical aspects that encompass my professional and social acclimation (and continued acclimation) as an assistant professor. What follows is an explication of the three:

1. diversity in dialogue but not in practice;
2. publish or perish paradigm; and
3. fighting to fit outside the box.

DIVERSITY IN DIALOGUE BUT NOT IN PRACTICE

While there remains a plethora of academic scholarship (Bonner, 2003; Cole & Barber, 2003) focusing on the educational pipeline of African American males, the experiences of African American male faculty remain under-researched (Bonner, 2004; Flowers & Jones, 2003; Heggins, 2004). Although notions of diversity and social justice have become prominent talking points within the scope of the academy, there still remain multiple levels of inequities for African American male faculty members, particularly those tenure-track professors employed at predominantly White institutions (Reyes & Louque, 2004). Concurrently, Bonner (2003) further asserts that African American male faculty members who are in the tenure process are less likely to be retained or awarded tenure in comparison to their White and Asian counterparts.

To be more specific, the premise of diversity in dialogue but not in practice is pertinent to institutions' conversations and policies that support a racially and ethnically diverse student body but do little to actively recruit and retain a diverse faculty of color (Alger, 1998; Bonner, 2004; Reyes & Louque, 2004). This is evident in my professional career, as I have been the only tenure-track African American male within the College and within a program area who admits a high percentage of African American students. Candid conversations with other scholars of color on campus have also voiced the need to expand the institution's commitment to true diversity that transcends the student population. Cole and Barber (2003) contend that continued diversification of faculty is a vital component of moving the institution in the right direction. In addition, Blackburn, Wenzel, and Bieber (1994) noted that "higher education institutions, as well as national research centers, need to focus on the experiences of faculty of color if we hope to understand the work environments needed to support creative talents" (p. 280). Above all, universities must be explicit about their development of diversity perspective and seek to ensure that all members of the campus community are clearly represented in order to truly diversify the practice and not just the dialogue of diversity in higher education.

109

PUBLISH OR PERISH PARADIGM

From the moment I received an assistant professor appointment there was an unspoken pressure to produce scholarship aligned with the narrowly defined interest of the individuals who would be evaluating my scholarly productivity. My research agenda, for instance, primarily focuses on academic identity development of gifted African American and Latino males. While my research is valued by my colleagues, I feel it is often seen as research outside the scope of "true" higher education research focuses (e.g., governance, leadership, organizational theory, educational law, to name a few). My expertise, in other words, often lends me to be typecast into ethnically specific research areas rather than discipline-specific areas. To better illustrate this point, as an assistant professor one of my first course appointments was Multicultural Education. Although I enjoyed the content of this course, there was no direct discussion prior to my employment about the availability of me instructing any other discipline specific courses.

In addition to my course assignments, this idea of being deemed an "ethnic specialist" is also experienced in my research focus. Even though it has been well documented that faculty of color bring with them innovative scholarship, the tenure and promotion structure does not always reward the value of such diverse thought in scholarship (Turner, 2000; Urrieta & Méndez Benavídez, 2007). As a result, faculty of color often experience an undue burden based on the dualistic nature of the tenure process. For example, I was often advised to focus a percent of my research in ethnically diverse journals and another percent in "mainstream" top tier journals. Such a message suggests that the counter-narratives inherent in the participants of my primary research area of African American and Latino males are not often published in "mainstream" top tier journals. This remains even more evident as Banda and I, who collaborate on several writing projects, debate the best journal to which to submit manuscripts. On one hand, one of our aims is to actively effect change within the scope of the educational paradigm, particularly to access and success of underserved populations in higher education. On the other hand, we also remain cognizant of our need to publish in top tier journals, which often prompt us to reframe the manner in which we write a manuscript. As a result, the publish or perish paradigm that remains is schizophrenic in nature due to the fact that one is constantly bombarded with multiple inner voices concerning the value of one's scholarship.

FIGHTING TO FIT OUTSIDE THE BOX

Upon my arrival in the academy, I quickly was prescribed the class(es) I would teach, the committees I would serve on, and the venues in which I should publish—all values that surely will be rewarded in the tenure and promotion structure. What I realized almost immediately is that the academy was trying to fit me into a box—a box that I was not sure if I fit or if I wanted to fit into. This regimented "box" was, at times, suffocating and almost always overwhelming in nature. I found that I resisted my need to bend, reshape, or be flexible—to redefine myself to fit in a very box that I had no design in. My struggle was to fight to fit outside the box instead of succumb a part of who I was as a person and who I wanted to grow as a scholar to fit into *their box*.

Laden and Hagedorn (2000) poignantly state that, "to date, faculty of color are expected to enter the academy and adapt themselves to the majority culture and norms that dominate their institutional workplaces" (p. 64). In essence, the institutional environment has a profound effect on the experiences of faculty of color as they either fight to be a part or fight to resist to be a part of the majority culture and norms of their institutions. This was particularly evident in my experience when I was assigned to serve on the diversity committee after only three days of employment. I quickly realized that the conversations of diversity were not about substantive issues regarding diversity within the college but rather ways in which we could implement a "band-aid" approach to such issues. Such a short-term approach was evident in our discussions pertinent to faculty search and hire practices and retention of faculty of color vis-à-vis faculty mentoring. Oftentimes, African American male tenure-track professors lack effective mentoring based on limited numbers of colleagues that share their ethnic or cultural backgrounds (Tillman, 2001). Building connections with mentors who allow one to gain access to other forms of capital necessary in the academy is vital, but often misunderstood when faculty of color who serve on diversity committees offer alternative perspectives. In other words, while I was often a voice of support for notions of diversity within the college I also provided a more critical lens on simplified solutions to complicated issues especially in regards to faculty mentoring. In reality, I tailored myself to temporarily fit into a box before truly voicing ideals that kept me anywhere but inside their prescribed box.

RECOMMENDATIONS

As highlighted in my narrative, the continued success of African American male faculty members starts within the context of the university. It is the institution's responsibility to facilitate a positive environment that fosters development and growth in all members of the faculty, particularly faculty of color. I offer five recommendations for university leaders to consider as they continue to find methods to support junior faculty members' positive acclimation to the campus environment.

1. *Provide transparency*: Make sure vital employment information (e.g., expectations for research, teaching, and service; campus resources; administrative policies and procedures) is available and easy to find for junior faculty.

2. *Mentoring is imperative*: Provide the opportunity for junior faculty to receive formal and informal mentoring.

111

3.   *Protect and support faculty*: Protect junior faculty, particularly faculty of color, from excessive teaching, advising, and service assignments. Offer opportunities to discuss the importance of how to balance all aspects of the faculty experiences. Do not create a "sink or swim" environment for junior faculty.

4.   *Value diverse research*: Prevent the undervaluing and short-changing of diverse research agendas of faculty of color.

5.   *Social support*: Investing in junior faculty members and helping them acclimate to the institutional community by providing them with transitional services. These services could include assistance with housing, social/professional networking, and other community related opportunities (i.e., church, clubs, or recreational sports). Consequently, an increased emphasis on faculty social transition can influence their productivity and feelings of connection to the institution.

CONCLUSION

This narrative inquiry via my explication of a series of dialogues with Banda has ignited a cognitive consciousness to the reality of the academy. Consequently, such conversations have prompted me to be more critical of how I examine and reflect on the professional and personal struggles that I continue to encounter as an assistant professor. This open dialogue has also ignited my need to voice the counter-narrative of what faculty of color experience in the academy. I am grateful for the opportunity to have a colleague who serves as a sounding board and provides a level of guidance that is often void in my campus community. Tuitt, Hanna, Martinez, Salazar, and Griffin (2009) assert that collective experiences "ensure that no one voice remain[ed] isolated or exposed" (p. 67). The changing complexion of the academy suggests that the voices of Black faculty can no longer be isolated and that the voices of majority faculty can no longer be the only voices exposed. Counter-narratives via the experiences of Black faculty must do more than just live the literature but seek to rewrite and reframe the literature on our experiences in the academy.

REFERENCES

Alger, J. B. (1998). Minority faculty and measuring merit: Start by playing fair. *Academe*, *84*, 71.

Ambrose, S., Huston, T., & Norman, M. (2005). A qualitative method for assessing faculty satisfaction. *Research in Higher Education*, *46*(7), 803–830.

Andrews, Molly, Squire, Corinne, & Tambokou, Maria (Eds.). (2008). *Doing narrative research*. London: Sage.

Antonio, A. L. (2002, September/October). Faculty of color reconsidered: Reassessing contributions to scholarship. *Journal of Higher Education*, *73*(5), 582–602.

Antonio, A. L. (2003, November/December). Diverse student bodies, diverse faculties. *Academe, 89*(6), 14–17.

Blackburn, R., Wenzel, S., & Bieber, J. P. (1994). Minority vs. majority faculty publication performance: A research note. *Review of Higher Education, 17*, 217–282.

Bonner, F. A. II. (2003). The temple of my unfamiliar: Faculty of color at predominantly White institutions. *Black Issues in Higher Education, 20*(18), 49.

Bonner, F. A. II. (2004). Black professors: On the track but out of the loop. *Chronicle of Higher Education Review, 50*(40), B11.

Cole, S., & Barber, E. (2003). *Increasing faculty diversity: The occupational choices of high-achieving minority students*. Cambridge, MA: Harvard University Press.

Defleur, M. L. (2007). Raising the question #5 what is tenure and how do I get it? *Communication Education, 56*(1), 106–122.

Diggs, G. A., Garrison-Wade, D. F., Estrada, D., & Galindo, R. (2009). Smiling faces and colored spaces: The experiences of faculty of color pursing tenure in the academy. *The Urban Review, 41*(4), 312–333.

Flowers, L. A., & Jones, L. (2003). Exploring the status of black male faculty utilizing data from the national study of post secondary faculty. *Journal of Men's Studies, 12*, 3–13.

Hagedorn, L. S. (2000). Conceptualizing faculty job satisfaction: Components, theories and outcomes. In L. S. Hagedorn (Ed.), *What contributes to job satisfaction among faculty and staff?* (105, Spring ed., pp. 5–20). San Francisco: Jossey-Bass.

Heggins, W. J. (2004). Preparing African American males for the professoriate: issues and challenges. *Western Journal of Black Studies, 28*(2), 354–365.

Jackson, J. F. L. (2003). Toward administrative diversity: An analysis of the African American male educational pipeline. *Journal of Men's Studies, 12*, 43–60.

Josselson, Ruthellen (2006). Narrative research and the challenge of accumulating knowledge. *Narrative Inquiry, 16*(1), 3–10.

Laden, B. V., & Hagedorn, L. S. (2000). Job satisfaction among faculty of color in academe: Individual survivors or institutional transformers. In L. Hagedorn (Ed.), *New directions for institutional research*, (Vol. 105, pp. 57–66). San Francisco: Jossey Bass.

Moore, J. L., III. (2000). Counseling African American men back to health. In L. Jones (Ed.), *Brothers of the academy: Up and coming Black scholars earning our way in higher education* (pp. 248–261). Herndon, VA: Stylus.

Reyes, L. Q., & Louque, A. (2004). The absence of diversity in the academy: Faculty of color in educational administration programs. *Education, 125*(2), 213–221.

Stanley, C. A. (2006, Winter). Coloring the academic landscape: Faculty of color breaking the silence in predominantly white colleges and universities. *American Educational Research Journal, 43*(4), 701–736.

Tillman, L. C. (2001). Mentoring African American faculty in predominantly White institutions. *Research in Higher Education, 42*, 295–325.

113

Tinto, V. (1997). Colleges as communities: Exploring the educational character of student persistence. *Journal of Higher Education, 68*, 599–623.

Tuitt, F., Hanna, M., Martinez, L. M., Salazar, M., & Griffin, R. (2009). Teaching in the line of fire: Faculty of color in the academy. *Thought & Action: the NEA Higher Education Journal, 16*, 65–67.

Turner, C. S. (2000, September/October). New faces, new knowledge. *Academe, 86*(5), 34–37.

Urrieta, L. Jr., & Méndez Benavídez, L. (2007). Community commitment and activist scholarship: Chicana/o professors and the practice of consciousness. *Journal of Hispanic Higher Education, 6*, 222–236.

Chapter 11

Engaging Mentoring Relationships in Academia

Hard Lessons Learned

Buffy Smith

INTRODUCTION

I dropped to my knees and began to cry after reading the official letter from my university that I was granted tenure and promoted to associate professor. Only God and I knew the true meaning behind the tears. I had finally achieved a goal that started approximately 16 years ago in graduate school. I was physically and emotionally exhausted from all the sacrifices I made and challenges I endured during this academic journey. In reading the letter, I was able to exhale and let go of some of my insecurities and fears. I was now free to be all of me in the academy.

In graduate school, I could not experience such freedom because I had to deal with issues related to my race, social class, gender, and sexual orientation. In addition, I am an extremely shy and introverted individual, which contributed to my lack of social capital in graduate school. I failed to recognize that not attending "happy hours," or professors' house parties and other department social events would have a negative impact on my overall graduate school experience.

EARLY FOUNDATIONS

Although it was never my intent to be reclusive, I now realize that is probably how I came across to my peers and professors. Luckily, I was also perceived as affable and funny. In fact, some peers told me they could not believe I was both friendly and anti-social. However, I have always lived with contradictions in my life. I grew up in public housing in the inner city of Milwaukee. I was on welfare (AFDC) but I always remember my mom working a minimum wage job and taking classes for different certificate programs. My mother, brother, and I attended church with my grandmother, who served as a co-parent with my mother.

My grandmother was a former sharecropper and domestic servant from Mississippi. She had only a sixth grade education but her vast wisdom could not be measured through formal education degrees. She expected me to love and serve God and do well in school. Both my mom and grandmom wanted me to go to college. I had a loving and supportive family but they did not have the knowledge or resources to prepare me for college. Although I came from a poor family, we valued education and had a strong work ethic. This might seem like a contradiction for some people, but it was my reality.

I did not know the proper procedures for applying to college and I only applied to one local university. I was admitted to the university through a program that helps low-income, first-generation college students and students of color. During my first year, I struggled academically and socially. I did not begin to adjust to college until my sophomore year. Eventually, I graduated with a B.A. in sociology and my mom was thrilled and proud of me. Unfortunately, my grandmom could not comprehend and appreciate the achievement because she suffered from Alzheimer's and ovarian cancer.

THE GRADUATE SCHOOL EXPERIENCE

I dedicated my B.A. degree to my grandmother. I was going to graduate school to earn a Ph.D., and I would dedicate that degree to my mother. When I arrived at graduate school, several faculty members told all of us, Ph.D. candidates, how lucky we were to be in the number one ranked sociology department. However, I did not feel lucky; I was scared, intimidated, and alone. It was the first time I moved to another city away from my family. There were few Blacks in the department and I could not easily identify people's social class of origin or sexual orientation. I felt a sense of alienation because my race was not fully embraced by the Lesbian Gay Bisexual Transgender Queer (LGBTQ) community, my social class by Whites, and my sexual orientation by Blacks. I was a floater among the different social groups.

My initial contact with some of my peers was intimidating as they shared their family and social class backgrounds. I was a minority not just because of my race, but also because I was a Black gay woman from a low-income background. Of course, this was not my first experience being the only Black person in a classroom but the insecurities about my academic abilities intensified during graduate school. My peers talked about concepts and theories I had never studied in my undergraduate program. I felt I was incapable of earning a Ph.D. My response to feeling inadequate was to distance myself from members in the department. I did not perceive the department as welcoming and affirming of all my identities and I decided not to impose myself on them. It appeared we had entered into a mutual agreement to have a peaceful coexistence. I felt the department would not kick me out, but if I wanted to leave, they would not try to stop me.

Imposter Syndrome

However, I could not quit, it was not how my mom and grandmom raised me. We are persistent women. I accepted the challenge and prepared for battle. I had to fight my fears and insecurities that attacked my self-esteem. I suffered from imposter syndrome. The "term imposter phenomenon is used to designate an internal experience of intellectual phonies, which appears to be particularly prevalent and intense among a select sample of high achieving women" (Clance & Imes, 1978, p. 241). I told myself constantly the department did not make a mistake by admitting me to the program. Although I might have benefited from affirmative action, that did not mean I did not have the intellect to succeed in graduate school.

In my program, I had to take preliminary exams in two different subfields of sociology. I failed both of them. This was a big test of my faith. I had to bear the shame of everyone in the department knowing I failed both exams. I was able to endure this major setback because I had experienced the greatest loss in my life a few years earlier when my grandmother passed away. If I was able to survive that pain and hurt, I knew I could survive all future disappointments in life. It did not matter how many times I would have to retake the prelims, I could not quit; it was not in my family's DNA.

The Hidden Curriculum and Social Capital

As I began to open up and share my pain about failing the prelims to friends in the department, I realized that most people formed study groups to prepare for the prelims. At that moment, I felt there was a hidden curriculum of graduate school that I did not know. The hidden curriculum refers to the unwritten norms, values, expectations, and rules of the institution (Apple, 1990; Bourdieu, 1986; Margolis, Soldatenko, Acker, & Gair, 2001; Smith, 2013). I was curious and wanted to know as much as I could about the hidden curriculum. I quickly discovered two of the hidden rules: (1) social capital is important and (2) mentors can help you navigate the graduate school process.

According to James Coleman (1988), social capital represents the information and resources that are shared among individuals in relationships or social networks. I did not understand why social capital was important. I was socialized to believe hard work was the path to success, now I was being told I should spend more time building relationships if I wanted to thrive in graduate school. As a shy and introverted individual, building social capital is a challenge, but I started accepting dinner invitations and attending house parties and "happy hours." I noticed that once I started socializing more with my peers, they would reveal more "insider knowledge" about the program to me. For example, I learned which professors were receiving large grants and looking for graduate students to hire as research assistants.

As I stretched myself beyond my comfort zone the more insider information I received from my peers. I entered the program without funding. As a result, I had various campus jobs, for example, cleaning bathrooms at the student center, entering survey data, and shelving books at the library. However, once I started building social capital with some of my peers they explained to me the process of obtaining a teaching assistantship and project assistantship. I used the same techniques to increase my social capital with the professors in the department. I attended their brown bag discussions. I scheduled meetings with them to talk about their research projects. I asked a few of them to serve as my mentors and they agreed. I was now feeling more connected to the program. I wasted many years thinking I had to do everything alone and I missed many opportunities in the process. As I graduated from graduate school, I vowed not to make the same mistakes when I became a junior faculty member.

JOB SEARCH

As an openly gay Black woman, I was fearful that I might not find an academic home that would fully embrace my multiple social identities. In fact, I had several uncomfortable campus interviews with different universities. For instance, a senior faculty member, White male, at one university actually told me to my face I was being interviewed as the "diversity hire" for the department. At another university, a member of the search committee, White female, politely assured me that it was okay to be gay as long as I did not "advertise my sexual preference." I was shocked by these responses because it was 2004, not 1964. After those experiences, I was doubtful that I would find a welcoming institution.

At first, I had many reservations about whether a Catholic university, which had an affirmative action statement that claimed the university did not discriminate based on sexual orientation, would be a good institutional fit for me. However, during my campus interview, I did not perceive any judgment, fear, or resistance to my multiple social identities. It was obvious I was a Black woman and I am confident that my male shirt, shoes, short buzz haircut, and masculine walk fit a stereotypical depiction of a gay woman. Yet, no one with whom I interviewed appeared to care. In addition, I was told I would be assigned a mentor in the department. Of course, I accepted the position and moved to a neighboring state. I was now six hours from my family of origin.

MY JOURNEY AS A JUNIOR FACULTY MEMBER

As a newly minted Ph.D., I was determined I would not make the same mistakes I made during graduate school. I was intentional about creating a sense of community in my department. I invited my chair and mentor, both wonderful White women, to meet my mom and have dinner with us at my apartment. I was forcing myself to go beyond my comfort zone in order to transition into my new life in academia. I attended public lectures, receptions, faculty meetings, and student-sponsored events, as many as possible, in order to be "visible" on campus.

It was not easy, because my natural instinct in front of large crowds is to find a corner and try to become invisible and blend into the wall. However, it is impossible for a tall, large-bodied, Black gay woman not to stand out at a predominantly White university. Therefore, I embraced all of my "uniqueness" and became more comfortable with being uncomfortable. Peers and students quickly rewarded my efforts. I noticed they also extended their comfort zones to reach out to me. I was able to create stronger social connections with peers and students as a result of having more open and honest conversations with them. I found and worked with colleagues who were committed to doing the hard labor that is required to sustain an affirming and inclusive learning and working environment.

The Importance of Mentoring

Many scholars have written about how mentoring influences the success of junior faculty of color (Dixon-Reeves, 2003; Moody, 2004; Stanley & Lincoln, 2005; Tillman, 2001; Turner, González, & Wood, 2008). My formal and informal mentors were the most important colleagues who helped me to understand and navigate the hidden curriculum of the university. In addition, they provided me support and strategies for managing the impact of institutional racism, sexism, and heterosexism. I was assigned an extraordinary mentor in the department who provided critical feedback on my rough drafts of articles, helped me interpret the guidelines for tenure and promotion in the faculty handbook and introduced me to her large social network. I learned many life lessons from her because she shared with me her joys and challenges of working in academia. She is a role model for how to balance family, teaching, research, and service commitments.

I believe we had a successful formal mentoring relationship because of the following reasons: (1) we had clear expectations of each other; (2) we respected each other as individuals with agency; (3) whenever there was a misunderstanding we would immediately address the issue; (4) we did not internalize critical feedback; (5) we trusted one another and were committed to developing our relationship. Overall, we were mindful of our different social identities but we did not allow those differences to prevent us from having conversations concerning race, social class, sexual orientation, and other sensitive topics. We were able to engage in honest and respectful discourse about any topic and that is why we are good friends today.

In addition to my formal mentor, I benefited from a team of informal mentors inside and outside my department. The informal mentoring team consisted of both junior and senior faculty. Informal mentors provided me with the opportunity to

119

hear multiple perspectives on an issue, which helped me make a more informed decision. I relied on my informal mentors to assist me with cultivating a sense of community on campus. It would have been easy for me to close the office door, conduct research and only come out to teach. However, I learned from my formal and informal mentors this would not signal that I am a friendly and an approachable person, and those two characteristics are important for building community. In order to thrive in higher education, I needed to be perceived as a team player. There is a close link between collaboration and collegiality, two traits on which we are informally evaluated during the tenure process.

The Value of Serving on Committees

Most mentors discourage junior faculty from joining too many university committees in order to protect their research and teaching time (Rockquemore & Laszloffy, 2008; Stanley, 2006). However, I joined several university committees as a way to signal my willingness to collaborate with other colleagues. It was my most authentic approach for building social capital. I enjoyed serving on committees because my grandmother and mother always emphasized the importance of service to God and community. Often, I felt out of place at receptions and other university social gatherings, but I was more comfortable serving on committees with other colleagues who shared the same passion for social justice issues. Although my mentors warned me not to join too many committees, I needed committees to help me feel connected to the university in a meaningful way. Overall, my desire for greater community connections was achieved through service to the university, engagement in local non-profit organizations and serving on committees for professional associations.

RECOMMENDATIONS

I learned valuable lessons as a graduate student and as a junior faculty member and I can now appreciate the journey. I have six major recommendations for fellow sojourners in academia.

- *Develop a senior faculty mentoring network*: Be open and honest about your fears, insecurities and challenges, allow your mentors to assist you on your journey.

- *Develop a junior faculty mentoring network*: Share your joys and challenges with each other, you need to hear the experiences of others who are going through the same process with you.

- *Do not suffer in silence*: Reach out early and often, when you need assistance, do not assume people do not care when they might be unaware that you are in need of assistance; utilize resources such as the faculty development center.

- *Build social capital*: Cultivate relationships in order to feel a sense of belonging on campus, be visible on campus; attend important receptions, faculty meetings, lectures, and other social events.

- *Learn the hidden curriculum*: You can learn the unwritten norms, values, and expectations of your university if you listen to the advice of your mentoring network; mentors will help you interpret and understand the institutional culture of the university.

- *Be authentic*: Be true to yourself during the tenure and promotion process, build social capital in a way that is aligned with your values, do things that will affirm your multiple social identities.

CONCLUSION

Although I barely survived graduate school, I am now thriving in my profession. I do not regret nor would want to change anything in my past. I truly believe I am where I am now, because I had to go through those struggles and challenges, everything happens for a reason and only lasts for a season. I am fully cognizant of my university's current institutional policies and practices that remain problematic and reproduce inequities in our society. However, I am also aware institutions are not perfect because flawed humans govern them. It is our shared collective responsibility to continue to challenge, question, and push our universities to become more equitable and just institutions.

As I continue to work on transforming my university, I cannot ignore the great progress I have witnessed at the institution. For instance, as a proud Black gay woman from a low-income background, I have cultivated a sense of community and received support and opportunities to thrive as a professional and as a person at a predominantly White, middle-class, Catholic university. Some people might think this is a contradiction, but it is my reality. However, I am not content with my individual achievements because I am mindful that my fate is interconnected to the destiny of all people from marginalized groups who still experience alienation, hostility, and other oppressive conditions in higher education. I must remain vigilant in creating more inclusive, equitable, and just learning and working environments.

REFERENCES

Apple, M. (1990). *Ideology and Curriculum* (2nd ed.). New York, NY: Routledge.

Bourdieu, P. (1986). The forms of capital. In J. G. Richardson (Ed.), *Handbook of theory and research for the sociology of education* (pp. 241–258). New York, NY: Greenwood.

Clance, P. R., & Imes, S. (1978). The imposter phenomenon in high achieving women: Dynamics and therapeutic intervention. *Psychotherapy Theory, Research and Practice, 15*(3), 241–247.

121

Coleman, J. (1988). Social capital in the creation of human capital. *American Journal of Sociology,* (Issue Supplement) *94*, 95–120.

Dixon-Reeves, R. (2003). Mentoring as a precursor to incorporation: An assessment of the mentoring experience of recently minted Ph.Ds. *Journal of Black Studies, 34*, 12–27.

Margolis, E., Soldatenko, M., Acker, S., & Gair, M. (2001). Peekaboo: Hiding and outing the curriculum. In E. Margolis (Ed.), *The hidden curriculum in higher education* (pp. 1–19). New York, NY: Routledge.

Moody, J. (2004). *Faculty diversity: Problems and solutions.* New York, NY: Routledge.

Rockquemore, K. A., & Laszloffy, T. (2008). *The Black academic's guide to winning tenure— without losing your soul.* Boulder, CO: Lynne Rienner Publishers.

Smith, B. (2013). *Mentoring at-risk students through the hidden curriculum of higher education.* Lanham, MD: Lexington Books.

Stanley, C. A. (2006). *Faculty of color: Teaching in predominantly white colleges and universities.* Bolton, MA: Anker Publishers.

Stanley, C. A., & Lincoln, Y. S. (2005). Cross-race faculty mentoring. *Change: The Magazine of Higher Learning, 37*(2), 44–50.

Tillman, L. C. (2001). Mentoring African American faculty in predominantly white institutions. *Research in Higher Education, 42*(3), 295–325.

Turner, C. S. V., González, J. C., & Wood, J. L. (2008). Faculty of color in academe: What 20 years of literature tells us. *Journal of Diversity in Higher Education, 1*(3), 139–168.

Chapter 12

The Critical Need for Faculty Mentoring

Say Brother, Can You Spare the Time?

Fred A. Bonner II

It was on a break from the activities we had implemented for the cohort of Black males attending the Samuel DeWitt Proctor STEM Collegiate African American Male Summit that my former doctoral advisee, who was participating as an invited speaker, reminded me of the diatribe I would always offer him when he talked to me about his career intentions and the critical milestones he needed to achieve in order to set his trajectory on an arc that would bend toward tenure, promotion, full professor and endowed chair in a "Research One" institution. Being the proud Generation Xer and my penchant to embrace everything "80s," it was his reminder of my typical response when he would come to me for these mentoring talks. It was the wisdom of my fellow Texan and sage Deborah or, as she is more commonly known, "Debbie" Allen that I would use to initiate my consultation sessions. Debbie's scene in the opening montage for the television series *Fame* depicted her in the role of her character dance teacher Lydia Grant admonishing her students at the New York City High School for the Performing Arts: "You got big dreams? You want fame? Well, fame costs, and right here is where you start paying." My adapted version of Grant's words typically was, "If you want to get to an R1, if you want to be tenured and promoted? If you ultimately want to become a full professor and endowed chair? Well, all those tickets have a price and right now you can't afford the fare! The beauty is I am here to help you to build your capital in order to purchase those tickets."

I view my role as mentor not only to be part and parcel of my responsibilities as a faculty member, but also I view mentoring to be perhaps the single most important role that I play as a faculty member. The time-honored verities that frame the very existence of those who seek to occupy space in the academy, namely teaching, research, and service, are the critical components that must be attended to if faculty members are to reach the highest rung on the faculty career ladder, achieving both promotion and tenure.

For the faculty member of color, all too often, we find ourselves negotiating this climb on a ladder that presents myriad obstacles (e.g., missing and slippery rungs) that make their ascent at best challenging. Thus, from the onset of a pro-fessional life in academe what becomes readily apparent to the faculty member of color is that strict adherence to the "rules of engagement" followed by White faculty peers might not assure a successful ascent. Theirs is an academic life that requires some "nuanced" as well as "culturally specific" strategies to insure that they too reach the highest professional rungs. One of the critical factors that I have found to consistently make a difference in the lives of junior faculty mem-bers of color, particularly related to their successful movement along the pro-motion and tenure pathway, has been having prolonged and persistent access to a *mentor*.

The title of this chapter references the American song from the Great Depres-sion era, "Buddy, Can You Spare a Dime?" What this tune conveys is the sense of urgency that legions of Americans faced, with the challenges of a profoundly challenging financial future, but the glimmer of hope for some sense of relief that could be provided by a compatriot who could afford (i.e., spare) to lend the individual some financial assistance. I see many parallels between faculty mem-bers of color in contemporary contexts faced with what they potentially perceive to be an uncertain future in academe and the uncertainties that Americans faced during the Great Depression. It is not my intent to be overly *grim* or approach the tenure and promotion process from a deficit-based perspective by using this metaphor; my purpose is to convey the essential role that individuals in a helping capacity play in assisting with the navigation through difficult times. The recom-pense for the sojourner who navigated the Great Depression terrain was money (i.e., dime), but for the traveler along the course in academe the remuneration required is *time*. Thus, my Scholarly Personal Narrative (SPN) begins from a very personal space with a story that is intimately connected to my focus on my own *emic* experiences as an African American male who has not only researched the experiences of faculty of color in postsecondary contexts, but also as an intrepid traveler who has been on a 16-year voyage attempting to make my way to the higher education *promised land*. This trek has been greatly facilitated by my men-tors who have served as guides that have been an ever-present force in keeping me apprised of impending dangers as well as motivated to keep moving when stalling or stopping seemed to be my only options.

So, what I have attempted to do for my colleagues who are junior faculty mentees is to spend time with them, listening to them talk about their triumphs and troubles experienced in academe. Hence I begin my SPN by sharing a story:

> The end of what I perceived to be another typical day in academe—my nor-mal routine of unloading my book bag, sorting through the mail, and decid-ing what culinary delight I would prepare for dinner was interrupted by the vibration of my cell phone and an incoming text message that read, "Are you busy?" The sender of this message—one of my former doctoral students

and newly minted assistant professor—was clearly intent on engaging in a conversation that very evening. My perception of his sense of urgency was based on my reply "I can call you after dinner" and his response—"Yes, I will wait by the phone!"

The conversation I engaged in with this young scholar centered on the many challenges he was experiencing as a first-year African American tenure-track faculty member. None of the issues he advanced in our vetting process did I find to be unique. And, what I was most pleased about was the mentoring relationship we had established; a relationship that transcended the role I played in his life as advisor and faculty member at the master's level, to faculty member and dissertation chair at the doctoral level.

Notwithstanding our long-standing mentoring relationship, what I found to be unique was not so much the content of our conversation or the fact that we were engaging in dialogue about the vicissitudes of faculty life. Unique was the fact that this relationship that I was engaging in with him was being recapitulated not only among my cohort of doctoral advisees who had transitioned into faculty positions subsequent to their graduation, but also in my relationships with legions of other doctoral students in myriad majors and programs across the university context and beyond who were also having the same experiences as neophyte faculty members.

In an article penned in the *Chronicle of Higher Education* titled "Black Professors: On the Track But Out of the Loop," I joined the conversation about faculty of color that many of my peers (Stanley, 2006; Thompson & Louque, 2005; Turner & Meyers, 2000) had been consistently engaging in at that point. Perhaps one of the most salient discussions I uncovered across their empirical findings was the narrative centered on the "added tax" often appended to Black faculty that spoke to the unspoken overabundance of mentoring support they often provided to their students, particularly to their students of color. From colleagues who are external to the Black faculty experience, "Just tell them you are not available" is commonly advanced as the panacea perceived to cure all ills. Yet, it's that feeling of being conflicted caused by the head's stern admonishment to protect yourself from time-consuming tasks like mentoring, and the heart's wise counsel to support those who might be retained simply because you cared enough to affirm them, that causes the faculty member of color the most angst (Bonner, 2004; Smith, 2004; Stanley, 2006; Turner & Myers, 2000). In regards to this dichotomous view of the role that mentoring plays often found to exist between faculty of color and their White counterparts, I liken my experience to Kevin Costner's character in the movie *Field of Dreams*, "If you build it they will come." However, what I often find eerily parallel to his character's experience is the feeling that I too am the only one who can hear the words or even more poignantly understand their implications.

125

Hence, the scholarship I have chosen as background to foreground my SPN includes the *Chronicle of Higher Education* article I previously mentioned as well as two additional publications—my book chapter "The Temple of My Familiar" and opinion editorial piece "Wade in the Water: A Contemporary Metaphor." Across these works are five common themes that serve to frame the mentoring discussions I engage in with junior faculty, especially faculty members of color. Each theme is treated in turn and supported by my personal narrative to provide an added dimension of authenticity to how it is experienced and operationalized in "real" world settings.

THEME ONE: PROVING YOURSELF OVER AND OVER

> Many African-American faculty members see themselves caught in a never-ending cycle of having to prove their competence as intellectuals. The literature on the experiences of minority professors shows that many believe that they must work twice as hard as other faculty members to get half as far.
>
> (Bonner, 2004)

As a faculty member of color, but more pointedly as an African American man who is occupying space and playing the role of professor in academe, I am ever mindful of the lessons in living that my parents, grandparents, and community shared with me during my developmental years as a means of fostering my learning growth and development. Notwithstanding the context, the lessons were always infused with a clear message conveying the need to be "ever mindful" of my status as an African American male. For me, the most indelible imprint that these teachings made was on my thinking related to how I had to orient myself to take on a world that had already been primed to view me as at best as "minor"ity and at worst as deficient. So I learned very early that waiting on "fair" treatment would cause you to miss out on doing the necessary work to generate the "fare" needed to take you to your next station in life. Said differently, by looking for life's situations to treat you fairly, you potentially lose sight of the necessary work that is required to generate the capital necessary to provide you passage to the next station in life. Thus, refrains such as "You must work twice as hard to get half as far" became a regular staple in my developmental diet. So, bringing these lessons forward and using them as fodder to support my mental well-being in the academy has been as natural as breathing.

Although I have been able to translate these lessons imparted to me by family into a sense of strength and resolve to take on the challenges presented to me by the academy, for many faculty members, especially newly minted faculty of color who are negotiating multiple and competing forces that shake them at their very foundations, they too draw on the sage advice received from family members on how to navigate perilous terrain. Thus, my mentoring advice for this cohort typically involves me sharing some of these life lessons, and to my surprise I often find that they too reveal the sage wisdom imparted to them by the elders from their communities as well. What I share is that these affirmations used in their personal spaces to make life more manageable are also useful in their professional spaces to make life more manageable; essentially they are invoking the same strategies but using them in a different context. In the offline conversations that I have with faculty of color—those behind-closed-door conversations that allow me to "switch into the code" that eschews pretense and the need for a veneer, I can engage in "real talk" about the "real experience" of being a person of color in academe. However, for these private times I have with Black faculty I am able to extend my cultural range of motion to draw on wisdom received from my community and family mentors who during my formative years imparted lessons from the schoolhouse to the Sunday school classroom.

The beauty of these mentoring exchanges I have with these junior faculty members, particularly African American and Black faculty who grew up in similar households and family traditions, is that we have a shared understanding of the meaning of these lessons; thus, what I help them to do is to frame these expressions in a way that they can use for empowerment and to fortify their resilience during their times of *Sturm und Drang*. The point of departure for a conversation about developing a dossier for tenure and promotion might begin with a discussion of the rudiments necessary to present a successful package (e.g., candidate statement, external reviewers, teaching evaluations). However, before the discussion concludes it is not uncommon for me to deviate from the path in order to read a guidepost that offers additional direction that I am able to infuse into the mentoring conversation to provide additional direction. These guideposts have signs affixed to them with some of the age-old lessons I have been alluding to that say things like "This joy that I have, the world didn't give it to me—the world didn't give it and the world can't take it away"—straight from Archie Dorsey's lips, our church musician at Macedonia Baptist Church in Linden, Texas, during my elementary and secondary school years. What on the surface appears to be simply a gospel tune, on a deeper level what it is for me in these mentoring spaces is a tool to help these junior scholars transgress what can be at times culturally, racially, and spiritually oppressive contexts. According to hooks (1994):

> Many of the issues that we continue to confront as black people—low esteem, intensified nihilism an despair, repressed rage and violence that destroys our physical and psychological well-being—cannot be addressed by survival strategies that have worked in the past. I insisted that we needed new theories rooted in an attempt to understand both the nature of our contemporary predicament and the means by which we might collectively engage in resistance that would transform our current reality.
>
> (p. 67)

127

THEME TWO: PROVIDING THE ENTERTAINMENT

> I had listened to my nonminority colleagues in nearby offices as they engaged in similar conversations with students. Their discussions centered on issues of academic expectations and rigor. Not once had I heard their students talk about the enjoyability of courses. It was as if they could satisfy students by providing knowledge, while for me the bar was raised. Not only was I to convey academic content, but I also had to entertain students. One of my colleagues echoed my feeling: "I don't have the luxury of coming to class with just a book and a smile, like some of my nonminority colleagues. I have to 'flash and dash' them with media and PowerPoint, lest they view me as lazy and incompetent." Another said ruefully, "It would be nice to sit back and just enjoy teaching without all of the extra pressures of trying to be an entertainer, but I guess this is not my lot."
>
> (Bonner, 2004)

Since the publication of the *Chronicle* article, I have had to defend my perspective regarding how I have experienced this particular theme more than any of the others combined. Often, the articulated cause of the angst for the individuals who have challenged me has typically stemmed from their desire to share that my assessment of the travails experienced by Black professors related to student expectations in the classroom are not unique to this cohort. "Well Dr. Bonner, White faculty also must attend to students' expectations in the classroom, I don't see how this is unique to Black faculty members." Inasmuch as I would like to trip the light fantastic back to the era in which I came of age—the 1980s—and offer a response only fitting a Spike Lee acolyte, "It's a Black thing and you just wouldn't understand," I instead pursue the academic pathway to lead the questioning agent to a place to trying to better understand the nuanced lives that Black faculty live in academe that are always just slightly off center when it comes to the congruence with how faculty life "is" experienced by their White peers and "should be" experienced by them. My narrative and sometimes diatribe uses as the wind beneath its wings discussions of Smith's (2004) chapter titled "Black Faculty Coping with Racial Battle Fatigue: The Campus Racial Climate in a Post-Civil Rights Era" as well as Stanley (2006), Tuner and Myers (2000), and Thompson and Louque (2005).

By stating my position and defending my stance on this theme, I am able to provide some direction to Black faculty mentees who too will potentially have to explain why their relationships with the academy are different from the relationships maintained by their White counterparts? For us, our realities are captured in Smith's (2004) commentary about the experiences of Black faculty who interface with White administrators in the college and university context who are oblivious to the unique experiences that Black faculty have in the college teaching and learning setting. He posits:

> Unfortunately and all too often, White university administrators downplay the race-based stress that African American professors experience at the classroom, department, university, and community level. More specifically, administrators fail to take seriously the level of physiological, psychological, and emotional stress experienced by African American teachers who are assigned classes of predominantly White students.
>
> (p. 179)

I heard the words of Dr. Etta Hollins during my 1996 summer experience in the minority doctoral fellowship program at Washington State University loud and clear. She said to us in unequivocal terms, "You should never let someone get out in front of you and tell your story, be prepared to situate yourself and explain to others how you are situated in your respective fields." My connection to this particular theme is one of those instances in which I have truly felt that I have had to "get out in front of 'them'" and tell my story of how I have uniquely experienced it—whether the masses believe it or not, I am comfortable in embracing my own truth. And, for junior Black faculty, they also have to be resolute in their stance.

In my mentoring conversations, again I tend to draw on my foundational teachings from home and church. Another favorite expression that also links me to my upbringing in the Baptist Church that I find myself sharing with junior faculty, another message from the guideposts, is the refrain, "Faith is the substance of things hoped for . . .," which is not only an excerpt from the Book of Hebrews but a cynosure for the Black community. What this biblical passage invokes for me, and I believe for many other African Americans, is that the belief in the ephemeral and superordinate, that cannot always be assessed, touched, or measured in objective terms, is no less valid than the objective reality we are taught to embrace as members of the academy.

THEME THREE: BEING KEPT OUT OF THE LOOP

> No faculty member can be successful without establishing professional networks—that is, being included in the higher-education loop. Unfortunately for many African-American faculty members, gaining access to the loop is difficult, if not impossible. New professors typically get into the loop through their advisers, mentors, and more-established colleagues. But many African-American faculty members have no one to help them make connections. Many of us have felt excluded from networks since graduate school, when professors chose nonminority students to write papers or

make presentations with them, ignoring minority students with equally high grades.

(Bonner, 2004)

What I see as one of the true benefits of being a faculty member of color in contemporary contexts is that, although there remains a tremendous amount of work to do be done regarding issues of diversity and race, some measured progress has been made since my matriculation and graduation from graduate school in the late 1990s. Perhaps what I have witnessed as the most noted change has been the increase in the number of people of color in general and Blacks in particular who have joined the ranks of higher education. It has been within the past five years that I served on a few dissertation committees in which the makeup of the group was comprised of all Black faculty members. I can remember on one occasion sitting in the small conference room at the predominantly White research institution in which I served as an administrator and professor waiting for the student to present his dissertation proposal, and found myself struck by the presence of my ebony- and mocha-hued compatriots who were all assembled for the purpose of assisting this neophyte scholar to cross the academic finish line. I reflected of my own experience as a doctoral student more than a decade prior to this occasion, and I thought, "How happy I would have been to simply have at least one Black professor."

Although I would categorize this experience as revealing some marked signs of progress, I am not naive in my understanding of the bigger issues that impact faculty of color in general and Black faculty in particular as they engage with academe. If we problematize and deconstruct the notion of the Black faculty presence in postsecondary education, we readily see that wide disparities exist between these faculty members and their White counterparts as well as deep chasms across the different faculty ranks (i.e., assistant, associate, and full). Also, when an exploration of the representation of faculty of color in certain disciplines is undertaken, very quickly we see the abysmal representation in key fields of endeavor such as science, technology, engineering, and mathematics (STEM). Hence my celebrations of these gains are always tempered.

Several years ago I submitted a proposal to the Association for the Study of Higher Education (ASHE) conference that focused on Black faculty narratives, primarily through counter-storytelling. The session included my counter-story along with narratives shared by Mary Howard-Hamilton, Robin Hughes, Michael Jennings, Lori Patton, and Christine Stanley. Each scholar unfolded a story to reveal their "take" on academe experienced via their own self-authored negotiations. A highlight of the session was Mary Howard-Hamilton's talk about the "leaky" pipeline for Black faculty in higher education. After a bit of commentary related to the tenuous state of affairs that existed for this population, she asked the audience—which was based on my non-empirical observation to be approximately 40% Black/African American—to participate in a brief exercise. In her always calming and confident tone, she asked the audience members to "Please stand if you are a graduate student," which she then followed by asking, "Please stand if you are an assistant professor," and then followed the same questioning route by asking for associate and then full professors. What was striking about this exercise is how the numbers of individuals who stood in representation of their particular group slightly dwindled at the front end of the exercise between the graduate student and assistant professor cohorts but had dropped exponentially toward the end of the activity when the full professors in the room were asked to stand. While almost two dozen individuals stood in representation of the graduate school contingency, only one—Christine Stanley—stood in representation of the full professors in the room, excluding Dr. Howard-Hamilton.

Is the cause of Black faculty "leaking" from the pipeline solely attributable to their inability to access critical networks? This question begs a reasoned and principled response if we are to properly identify the root cause(s) of this problem. Even though research indicates the lack of access to professional and social networks, we know that the absence of these liaisons can have a debilitating impact on a faculty career. According to Diggs, Garrison-Wade, Estrada, and Galindo (2009), as well as Turner and Myers (2000) in their empirical investigation more than a decade ago:

> Faculty of color find themselves outside the informal networks of the department. A sense of isolation is among the most commonly reported problems in the literature as well as in our study. Although merit and autonomy are touted as institutional values in the academy, a major contributor to success in the professoriate is association with senior colleagues. Without such affiliation, faculty of color are isolated and struggle though the socialization process alone.
>
> (Turner & Myers, 2000, p. 24)

Therefore, for Black faculty, whether the metaphor speaks of loops or networks, the important statement that must serve as a precursor is "*included in* . . ." Though access to these networks might not be the panacea to cure the ills of a leaky pipeline, it does serve as an additional patch to mend an otherwise compromised system.

THEME FOUR: PLAYING TWO ROLES

Members of minority groups often have to engage in what sociolinguists call "code switching," moving back and forth between identities to succeed in two disparate worlds. Sometimes the switch has to take place very quickly, in as short a time as it takes to walk from your car to your office. Actions, behavior, language, persona all change as you turn off the rhythm-and-blues

131

music and turn on the academic mind-set. Many African-American faculty members form support networks with people outside of higher education: family and friends, folks living in the 'hood, members of their church, and acquaintances from the beauty shop or barbershop. With those people, one professor reported, he could jettison the burden of having to prove his academic prowess and enjoy the comforts of "just being black."

(Bonner, 2004)

One of my favorite quotes is taken from an Atlantic Monthly article penned by W. E. B. DuBois (1897). In this article, which was later included in his book The Souls of Black Folks, DuBois introduced his double consciousness theory that referenced the deep psychological challenges that African Americans faced in reconciling their dual identities as both African American and European. DuBois posited:

It is a peculiar sensation, this double-consciousness, this sense of always looking at one's self through the eyes of others, of measuring one's soul by the tape of a world that looks on in amused contempt and pity. One ever feels his two-ness,—an American, a Negro; two souls, two thoughts, two unreconciled strivings; two warring ideals in one dark body, whose dogged strength alone keeps it from being torn asunder.

(para. 3)

Learning to play the game of "identity hopscotch" happened for me far earlier than my initiation into the academy. As a Black child and now man living in America, particularly growing up in the rural South, understanding when to slide in and out of your racial identity expression had to become as second nature as slipping on your favorite winter coat. In the college and university context, especially in my role as a professor, my transitioning between codes was as much, if not more, about being true to self as it was about how I was being perceived by my colleagues and students. In a prefatory I completed for the *Journal of African American Males* titled "Negotiating the 'In-Between:' Liminality and the Construction of Racial Identity Among African American Male Collegians," I talked about the difficulties Black collegiate men had in attempting to frame their identities, especially when the dimensions of the portraits they painted of themselves were 11 x 14 renderings that society forced them to fit into a 3 x 7 frame. Thus, having the privilege to fully experience the panoply of cultural and ethnic identities is hardly ever an option. Much like the experience of the African American male in the postsecondary setting, so too do faculty of color, especially Black faculty, often feel the pressures of truncating aspects of their cultural selves to fit into templates that White academe deems appropriate.

It was in Grace-Dodge Hall at Teachers College that my graduate school classmate and best friend said to the audience during our presentation about the experiences of Black faculty in predominantly White institutions (PWIs), "I'm not so sure I am willing to become the person the academy expects me to come just to get tenure." I understood it then as a young junior faculty member and I more fully understand it now as a senior faculty member who is more than 15 years beyond the tenure and promotion stop on my career pathway. While hindsight might be 20/20, I am thankful that my ocular occlusion at that time was not so severe that it impeded my vision to see that throwing myself into the flames back then would later allow me to rise from the ashes.

THEME FIVE: FEELING UNWELCOME

Many women, members of cultural and ethnic minority groups, and many gay and lesbian people have found academe an inhospitable environment. African-Americans at predominantly white institutions, in particular, often stop hoping for anything more than toleration. Few universities offer a supportive infrastructure. Although some institutions have offices of minority affairs, those are typically designed to meet the needs of students; faculty members must fend for themselves.

(Bonner, 2004)

Michelle Obama in her senior thesis at Princeton University more than 30 years ago expressed her feelings of being "on the periphery" of the campus and never fully feeling a part of the institution. Much like First Lady Obama's expressions in her thesis, faculty of color in general, and Black faculty in particular, also struggle with feeling "at home" on their respective campuses. Turner and Myers (2000) talk about the "chilly climate" experienced by faculty of color in PWI contexts. In addition Kamau (1998) stated:

The metaphor "chilly climate" is a relatively new term which entered higher education in the last fourteen years. It was coined by Roberta M. Hall and Bernice Sandler in their widely acclaimed chilly "Climate Report" in 1986. They used the term to describe the subtle ambiance in which many small inequities can create a negative atmosphere for learning, teaching and for fulfilling professional roles on campus.

(p. 2)

While the literature on the chilly climate has become somewhat dated, unfortunately the actions associated with creating these campus contexts is just as problematic now as it was in the mid-1980s. What have evolved are the monikers and attendant descriptive terms that we use to try to explain this phenomenon. Now we employ terms like *critical race theory (CRT)* and *microaggression* to explain the marginalizing effect that higher education settings can exact on faculty of color. A

133

number of solutions have been advanced as plausible responses to reduce the chill in the air for these faculty cohorts. One of my favorite contemporary articles by Diggs, Garrison-Wade, Estrada, and Galindo (2009) speaks to the issue of climate and what might be done in particular to address the issue:

> The unofficial, informal space allows faculty of color to be "real"; to express themselves, share experiences and perspectives and vent and support each other in (cultural) ways that are not necessarily safe in the official, formal workplace. The existence of spaces such as these may help faculty of color cope with frustrations with the environment or school climate. This may, in turn, support both recruiting and retention efforts aimed at diversifying the academy. In summary, minority faculty members often bring more to the academic environment than various shades and colors. If institutional commitments to recruiting and retaining diversity are to be successful, such efforts should consider what it means for faculty of color to develop their professional identities within a traditional, white environment.
>
> (p. 331)

Adopting measures to adjust the climate control to reduce the chill in the air is essential if institutions are truly interested in not only recruiting but also retaining their faculty of color. In the higher education course that I teach, Assessing Educational Environments, I use Strange and Banning's (2001) book, in which they devote a chapter to the perceptual environment. The clearest message conveyed is that individuals uniquely experience the campus environment. What some view as a warm and supportive campus setting, others might view as cold and distant.

RECOMMENDATIONS

Below is a list of, albeit limited, recommendations that I offer based on my own experiences.

- Create opportunities for Black faculty to connect with peers in a "safe space" in which they can dialogue about their individual experiences of being a faculty member of color in academe. This addresses the "I am the only one" feelings that this cohort often reports.

- Identify and address the inherent pitfalls that Black faculty experience, such as the "double standard" students often operationalize related to faculty evaluations, as well as open hostility and racism in classroom engagements.

- Ensure that Black faculty is apprised of key conferences and organizations in their respective fields and also is providing access to resources in order for them to engage these events and groups.

- Provide forums for Black faculty to talk about their research and scholarship that will allow them to share the range of their interests, particularly culturally specific interests.

- Promote activities that are inclusive of Black faculty that welcome them to the department, college, and institution.

CONCLUDING THOUGHTS

The sermon delivered by the late Samuel DeWitt Proctor titled "Rising Above the Scratch Line" has become a regular part of my academic presentations. Given the focus of my research on marginalized populations across the P-20 educational continuum, it is incumbent on educators to help all learners rise above the "scratch line." Dr. Proctor's prophetic words are transcendent and have meaning and applicability in myriad contexts. Thus, I see it as my charge to help Black faculty to rise above the scratch line to accomplish their professional goals. I hear the words of the old gospel hymn that we often sang at church during the period of service referred to as the devotional. Typically led by one of the deacons or deaconesses of the church we would, through call and response, sing in a slow metered rhythm, "A charge to keep I have, a God to glorify . . ." And, through mentoring, I continue to keep my charge.

REFERENCES

Bonner, F. A. II. (2004). Black professors: On the track but out of the loop. *Chronicle of Higher Education Review, 50*(40), B11.

Diggs, G., Garrison-Wade, D., Estrada, D., & Galindo, R. (2009). Smiling faces and colored spaces: The experiences of faculty of color pursuing tenure in the academy. *The Urban Review, 41*(4), 312–333.

DuBois, W. E. B. (1897, August). Strivings of the Negro people. *Atlantic Monthly*. Retrieved May 8, 2014 from: http://www.theatlantic.com/past/unbound/flashbks/black/dubstriv.htm.

hooks, b. (1994). *Teaching to transgress: Education as the practice of freedom*. New York, NY: Routledge.

Kamau, N. M. (1998). Reconceptualizing chilly climate: Minority faculty in North American academe. Paper presented at the Third Annual National Conference, Lincoln, NE.

Smith, W. A. (2004). Black faculty coping with racial battle fatigue: The campus racial climate in a post-Civil Rights era. In D. Cleveland (Ed.), *A long way to go: Conversations about race by African American faculty and graduate students* (pp. 171–190). New York, NY: Peter Lang.

The Souls of Black Folk (1996, April). (Penguin Classics reprint [paperback] ed.). New York: Penguin Books.

Stanley, C. A. (Ed.). (2006). *Faculty of color: Teaching in predominantly White colleges and universities*. Boston, MA: Anker Publishing.

Strange, C., & Banning, H. (2001). *Educating by design: Creating campus learning environments that work*. San Francisco, CA: Jossey-Bass.

Thompson, G. L., & Louque, A. C. (2005). *Exposing the culture of arrogance in the academy: A blueprint for increasing Black faculty satisfaction in higher education*. Sterling, VA: Stylus Publishing.

Turner, C. S. V., & Myers, S. L., Jr. (2000). *Faculty of color in academe: Bittersweet success*. Boston, MA: Allyn & Bacon.

Chapter 13

Establishing Critical Relationships with Students

That's Not What White Professor "X" Told Us

Saundra M. Tomlinson-Clarke

After the successful completion of my dissertation defense, the only woman on my committee of four welcomed me to the *"three percent."* She was referring to women with earned Ph.D. degrees. I was then reminded by my committee members that the percentage of Black women with earned doctorates was lower. In the midst of the joy I experienced in accomplishing this educational milestone, I was keenly aware of how my critical relationships with faculty guided my development as a college student and prepared me for success as a graduate student. Critical relationships with faculty were instrumental to my socialization into the profession.

Reflecting on my lived experience 30 years later, the impact of the *"three percent"* has taken on a deeper meaning. Critical race theory (Ladson-Billings, 1998, 2005; Solórzano & Yosso, 2001) and the Dimensions of Personal Identity (Arredondo & Glauner, 1992; Arredondo, Toporek, Brown, Jones, Locke, Sanchez, & Stadler, 1996) provided a comprehensive theoretical framework for unpacking individual, cultural, and societal factors influencing my critical relationships established with faculty. Discourses related to social processes and institutional practices shaped my perceptions of the world and my interactions with others (Aguirre, 2010). Race, gender, and socioeconomic status have influenced who I am as a professional. I will reflect on the rewards, the challenges, and the lessons learned that shaped my realities and defined what I consider to be critical in establishing relationships with students as a Black, woman, tenured faculty member at a predominantly White, research university.

REFLECTIONS SHAPING MY REALITY

Early Influences

Growing up in a military family, my brother and I learned the importance of "following the chain of command," which translated into following the rules established by our parents. As third-generation college students, we were told the importance of deciding early whether we were merely *going to college* or making a commitment to *being a college student*. *Being a college student* involved taking responsibility for my learning, and seeking out opportunities to actively engage in self-discovery and personal growth. I quickly made the decision to be a college student. Because I always found my family relationships to be warm, caring, and supportive, I anticipated finding similar relationships in my educational experiences. This, however, was not always the case.

Establishing Critical Relationships as a Student: PWI and HBCU

As an undergraduate student on a predominantly White campus, I sought out a variety of collegiate experiences. As a student of the 1970s, we coalesced around issues of civil rights and anti-war. UMOJA, the Black Student Association, was a major presence on campus. *Umoja*, the Swahili word which means "*unity*," brought students of color and allies together for a common cause. Strong peer support was available from minority students on my campus as well as from minority students on other campuses in this city where race was a defining characteristic. Black faculty was underrepresented, and resulted in a noticeable absence of Black women faculty in my collegiate experience. Despite knowing the importance of establishing relationships with faculty, my first critical faculty–student relationship did not occur until my junior year after declaring a major. My advisor, who was a Black male, took a sincere interest in me. In addition to serving as my advisor, I was a member on his research team and worked under the direct supervision of a second year clinical psychology doctoral student, who also was a Black male. In my formal role as an undergraduate research assistant, I reviewed literature and collected data. I also was advised and guided by informal networks. My advisor made certain that I was prepared to pursue graduate study. This preparation did not translate into "hand holding and coddling," but rather began the process of socialization into the values of the profession. Both formal and informal faculty–student and student–student relationships established in college served to guide my personal and career development. Lessons learned from early relationships with family and with mentors in college included the importance of consistency, caring, and support as a foundation that motivated me toward increased educational attainment. Consistent across these critical mentoring relationships was an unwavering belief in my ability to succeed.

An absence of mentoring and poor mentoring is cited as reasons for the underrepresentation of racial-ethnic minority youth in the educational pipeline from high school to college and from college to graduate school (Johnson, Bradley, Knight, & Bradshaw, 2007; Samel, Sondergeld, Fischer, & Patterson, 2011). Faculty–student mentoring serves as a form of social capital, dictating how and to whom resources are distributed. Too often, racial-ethnic minority and women students are excluded from social supports and informal networks linked to student adjustment and success (Guiffrida & Douthit, 2010). The underrepresentation of minority faculty as well as historical legacies of exclusion contribute to feelings of alienation experienced by underrepresented students on predominantly White campuses (Felder, 2010; Harper, 2013). As a result, students of color and, in particular, Black students are more likely to feel a lack of respect from their professors, attribute perceived barriers and challenges to their ethnicity, and report less satisfaction with their studies when compared to White students (Lott & Rogers, 2011).

Attending a private Historically Black College and University (HBCU) for my master's degree provided me with the relational foundations that were often missing from my undergraduate experience at a predominantly White university (PWI). In contrast to the collegiate environment at a PWI, life at a HBCU more closely paralleled the supportive relationships that I experienced with my family. Rather than a focus on things, people and their well-being were deemed most important. Critical relationships that influenced my career were established with both men and women faculty, several who were White and perceived as allies. Common beliefs among faculty that I encountered in a historically Black college environment focused on a holistic approach to student development. There was a collectivistic orientation that was not present in my experience at a predominantly White university. These feelings of caring and support extended from the faculty to the students. I felt the "we" in my interactions with my peers and in my relationships with faculty. Immersed in an HBCU actualized the concept of "togetherness"—we were in this together, supporting one another as we matriculated toward our educational goals. Ally, ambassador, and master teacher are identified as faculty roles and responsibilities that contribute to graduate student success (Lechuga, 2011). These critical faculty–student relationships established at an HBCU became a defining experience in my development that has influenced my interactions with students today.

My reality was challenged, however, while attending a predominantly White research university for doctoral education. Not aware until arriving on campus that Blacks were not admitted to this university until the late 1960s was somewhat of a reality check. My lived experience at the institution brought back feelings as an undergraduate student. I often felt invisible to my professors, unable to develop meaningful relationships with faculty. The inability to develop critical relationships with White faculty is reported to be a common experience among Black students attending PWIs (Guiffrida & Douthit, 2010). However, different from my undergraduate experiences, graduate education involved smaller cohorts, and my feelings of alienation increased. Although I was privy to formal information sharing, with a few exceptions, I felt excluded from informal faculty–student interactions. On a few occasions, my peers would provide me with information they received from informal networks. Those peers tended to be White males, who probably did not see me as their competition. I often felt that many of the White faculty and graduate students did not perceive that my experiences connected to theirs. Despite multiple dimensions of my personal identity, I felt I was judged solely based on my salient characteristics of race, gender, and age. Possible dimensions of shared identity that might have built a closer rapport with peers and faculty were often ignored (Arredondo & Glauner, 1992).

During my doctoral education, I experienced an interaction with a client that illustrated the impact of race and gender in a racialized society. In an initial counseling session, the client looked shocked as I entered the room. As she struggled to disguise her reaction, she proceeded to tell me that "although I was probably very capable, she did not think that we would have a connection. After all, she was White and married, and I was Black and most likely not married." My salient characteristics influenced a quick judgment regarding my level of expertise as a counselor? Was it because I was Black, young, or a combination of visible characteristics that allowed her to assume that our relationship would not be effective? Whatever the reason, I was judged as lacking professional credibility. According to Sue and Zane (1987), the process of credibility involved two critical factors: (1) ascribed credibility and (2) achieved credibility. Ascribed credibility is the role or position that is assigned to you by others. Achieved credibility is acquired based on your training and level of skill. In this situation, the client perceived that my personal characteristics (ascribed credibility) affected my professional credibility, despite my level of training and skills (achieved credibility). From this situation I learned that my salient characteristics as a young, Black woman might affect perceptions of my professional expertise.

Given my level of cultural competence today, I would have processed the client's reaction with my supervisor rather than remaining silent and immediately acquiescing to demands for a White counselor. With an emphasis on multicultural supervision informed by a social justice agenda, this interaction was a teachable moment. Using critical race theory to process this exchange may have assisted the class in developing a deeper understanding of racial socialization in society (Ladson-Billings & Tate, 1995; Lee & Ahn, 2013), and the dynamics of contemporary and often subtle forms of oppression that are commonplace in the life of minority people (Sue & Sue, 2013).

Despite this experience, I was fortunate to have an advisor and dissertation chair who was an ally. His salient personal dimensions of identity were opposite of mine. He was a White man raised in the South and I was a Black woman raised in the North. I felt that I mattered—he took the time to know me as an individual. Personal dimensions of diversity and personal identity extend beyond visible characteristics and include family, religion, SES, beliefs, and experiences (Arredondo et al., 1996). He was one of the few White faculty members during that era that openly acknowledged the importance of multicultural competence in working across cultures. He understood the influence of race, gender, and

140

culture in society as well as the impact of institutional racism on students of color attending PWIs. His commitment to social justice strengthened our bond. My lived realities were acknowledged and I did not feel that I was stereotyped or misrepresented. He was invested in my future career. Regardless of race, a faculty member that is "genuinely interested in a doctoral student's research agenda, professional development, and degree completion" is important for success among African American graduate students (Felder, 2010, p. 458).

ESTABLISHING CRITICAL RELATIONSHIPS IN MY EARLY CAREER

In reflecting on my critical relationships, very few women in the academy have been part of my development as a professional woman. Critical relationships with women faculty, specifically Black women faculty, in my early development may have provided learning experiences from which I would have benefited. Students' expectations may differ as a function of faculty race and gender. Black faculty and specifically Black women faculty tend to engage in a disproportionately higher number of mentoring relationships than their White colleagues (Griffin, 2012). Mawhinney (2012) discussed her experiences as a Black female faculty member with *othermothering* of students. Due to their underrepresentation, women faculty of color and their lived experience continue to be underrepresented in universities and in the research literature, respectively (Turner, González, & Wong, 2011).

This is not to discount men as effective role models for women. I can certainly attest to the impact of men faculty as mentors in my professional development. Critical in my transition from student services to faculty was the mentoring I received from a Black male professor while working at a predominantly White research university. Interestingly, his mentor had been a Black woman on the faculty and administration at a PWI. Through this seminal relationship, I became more keenly aware of the values and priorities of the academy (Boyer, 1990). Support, encouragement, and feedback in negotiating the dynamics of the academy are key to a successful mentoring relationship (Griffin & Toldson, 2012). This lived experience reinforced to me that mentoring is developmental, and can occur at various stages of an individual's career.

LESSON LEARNED: ESTABLISHING CRITICAL FACULTY–STUDENT RELATIONSHIPS

I encountered a number of challenges as a Black and untenured faculty member teaching in a graduate program at a PWI. Some students approached me with the assumption that I needed to be "schooled" on the ways of academia and seemed to doubt that I was capable of performing the requirements of my position. Could a Black woman correct the sentence structure or grammar on a White student's

141

paper or dissertation without student protest? Could a Black woman provide a lecture on counseling appraisal instruments without having a White student yell out "That's wrong? That's not what Dr. X said." (The student did not realize at the time that she had confused her statistical terminology and remained adamant that I was delivering incorrect information to the class.) Clearly my knowledge and expertise was being questioned in front of a graduate class. Racialized expectations have been shown to influence students' perceptions of Black professors (Tuitt, 2011).

Sue and Sue (2013) discussed the impact of intentional and unintentional racial microaggressions on the psyche of the individual. Feeling the need to validate my reality, I conferred with Dr. X to see if I was wrong in my understanding of the concepts that I was teaching. Had I provided students with incorrect information? After speaking with Dr. X, I felt a sense of relief, yet a sense of anger. I was relieved and my confidence in my knowledge of the content area was restored. Anger emerged because I questioned my competence based on what one student said. How does a student feel such authority and privilege to openly challenge a professor in front of the class? Would that same student openly challenge a White professor, a male professor? My understanding of the perceptions that some students might have about me as a young, Black woman professor were crystallized as a result of that experience. Racial battle fatigue resulting from racial microaggressions, micro-insults, and micro-invalidations by colleagues and students were reported to be common experiences among Black faculty at PWIs (Pittman, 2012; Smith, Hung, & Franklin, 2011). Pittman (2012) noted the importance of addressing *interpersonal racial oppression* in creating safe campus climates for faculty as well as students.

RECOMMENDATIONS

Lived experiences as a student, in addition to my interactions with my students and faculty colleagues, have influenced what I consider to be important considerations in developing faculty–student relationships. Based on my reflections and lessons learned, I offer four recommendations for establishing critical relationships with students.

- *Seek out encouraging and reaffirming relationships*: Connect with supportive formal and informal networks that provide opportunities for continuous mentorship in your development as a faculty member.

- *Believe in students' ability to achieve academic and personal success*: Do not underestimate the value of critical faculty–student relationships throughout the educational pipeline. Encouragement empowers students and is likely to increase their educational aspirations, and overall success in life.

- *Assist students in demystifying the bureaucracy of the academy*: You can assist students in understanding the *dos* and *don'ts* of the academy. Through relationships with faculty, students can effectively negotiating the collegiate environment, while maintaining a positive and reaffirming self-identity.

- *Engage in critical self-reflection*: Take time to engage in reflection to guide your faculty role and responsibilities. Also, think carefully about the personal and professional characteristics that you possess (or may need to further develop) that aid in cultivating critical relationships with your students.

CONCLUSION

In the counseling profession, trust is basic to developing a genuine and caring relationship. I acknowledge that race, gender, class do matter and influence the perceptions and expectations of my colleagues and students (Griffin, 2012). My lived experience, inclusive of my teaching, service, and scholarship, has prepared me to address issues of race and culture within the context of equity and education in creating a supportive and caring learning environment and campus climate. I have developed the cultural competencies to address intentional and unintentional expressions of bias that interfere with learning and achievement (Sue & Sue, 2013).

Remembering the lessons taught to me by my parents and my critical relationships with faculty continue to guide me in the actions that I take with students. I follow the chain of command, respecting the hierarchy of the institution. I make the time to be available to students. I place emphasis on developing the strengths of the individual student, and provide learning opportunities that assist in maximizing students' personal and professional development. Through critical relationships established with students, my faculty responsibilities include:

1. providing academic advising and career guidance;
2. delivering quality teaching and learning experiences; and
3. socializing students into the norms and values of the profession.

In sum, engaging students, providing encouragement, support and feedback, and validating and valuing their experiences are critical in establishing effective faculty–student relationships that promote student development (Griffin & Toldson, 2012). Through faculty–student relationships, I strive to increase students' self-efficacy and belief in their ability to achieve success in their career and in life.

REFERENCES

Aguirre, A., Jr. (2010). Diversity as interest-convergence in academia: A critical race theory story. *Social Identities, 16*, 763–774.

Arredondo, P., & Glauner, T. (1992). *Personal dimensions of identity model*. Boston: Empowerment Workshops, Inc.

Arredondo, P., Toporek, R., Brown, S. P., Jones. J., Locke, D. C., Sanchez, J., & Stadler, H. (1996). Operationalization of the multicultural counseling competencies. *Journal of Multicultural Counseling and Development, 24*, 42–78.

Boyer, E. L. (1990). *Scholarship reconsidered: Priorities of the professoriate*. Princeton, NJ: Princeton University Press. The Carnegie Foundation of the Advancement of Teaching.

Felder, P. (2010). On doctoral student development: Exploring faculty mentoring in the shaping of African American doctoral student success. *The Qualitative Report, 15*, 455–474.

Griffin, K. A. (2012). Black professors managing mentorship: Implications of applying social exchange frameworks to analyses of student interactions and their influence on scholarly productivity. *Teachers College Record, 114*, 1–37.

Griffin, K. A., & Toldson, I. A. (2012). Reflections on mentoring for Blacks in the academia (Editor's commentary). *Journal of Negro Education, 8*, 103–105.

Guiffrida, D. A., & Douthit, K. Z. (2010). The Black student experience at predominantly White colleges: Implications for school and college counselors. *Journal of Counseling & Development, 88*, 311–318.

Harper, S. R. (2013). Am I my brother's teacher? Black undergraduates, racial socialization and peer pedagogies in predominantly white postsecondary contexts. *Review of Research in Education, 37*, 183–211.

Johnson, P. D., Bradley, C. R., Knight, D. E., & Bradshaw, E. S. (2007). Preparing African American counselor education students for the professorate. *College Student Journal, 41*, 886–890.

Ladson-Billings, G. (1998). Just what is critical theory and what's it doing in a nice field like education. *International Journal Qualitative Studies, 11*, 7–12.

Ladson-Billings, G. (2005). The evolving role of critical race theory in educational scholarship. *Race, Ethnicity and Education, 8*, 115–119.

Ladson-Billings, G., & Tate, W. F., IV. (1995). Toward a critical race theory of education. *Teachers College Record, 97*, 47–68.

Lechuga, V. M. (2011). Faculty-graduate student mentoring relationships: Mentor's perceived roles and responsibilities. *Higher Education, 62*, 757–771.

Lee, D. L., & Ahn, S. (2013). The relation of racial identity, ethnic identity, and racial socialization to discrimination-distress: A meta-analysis of Black Americans. *Journal of Counseling Psychology, 60*, 1–14.

Lott, B., & Rogers, M. R. (2011). Ethnicity matters for undergraduate majors in challenges, experiences, and perceptions of psychology. *Cultural Diversity and Ethnic Minority Psychology, 17*, 204–210.

Mawhinney, L (2012). Othermothering: A personnel narrative exploring relationships between Black female faculty and students. *Negro Educational Review, 62 & 63*, 213–232.

Pittman, C. T. (2012). Racial microaggressions: The narratives of African American faculty at a predominantly White university. *Journal of Negro Education, 81*, 82–92.

Samel, A. N., Sondergeld, T. A., Fischer, J. M., & Patterson, N. C. (2011). The secondary school pipeline: Longitudinal indicators of resilience and resistance in urban schools under reform. *High School Journal, 94*, 95–118.

Solórzano, D., & Yosso, T. J. (2001). Critical race and LatCrit theory and method: Counter-storytelling. *International Journal of Qualitative Studies in Education, 14*, 471–495.

Smith, W. A., Hung, M., & Franklin, J. D. (2011). Racial battle fatigue and the miseducation of Black men: Racial microaggressions, societal problems, and environmental stress. *Journal of Negro Education, 80*, 63–82.

Sue, D. W., & Sue, D. (2013). *Counseling the culturally diverse: Theory and practice* (6th ed.). Hoboken, NJ: John Wiley & Sons, Inc.

Sue, S., & Zane, N. (1987). The role of culture and cultural techniques in psychotherapy: A critique and reformulation. *American Psychologist, 42*, 37–45.

Tuitt, F. (2012). Black like me: Graduate students' perceptions of their pedagogical experiences in classes taught by Black faculty in a predominantly White institution. *Journal of Black Studies, 43*, 186–206.

Turner, C. S. V., González, J. C., & Wong, K. L. (2011). Faculty women of color: The critical nexus of race and gender. *Journal of Diversity in Higher Education, 4*, 199–211.

Contributors

Rosa M. Banda is Research Associate to the Samuel DeWitt Proctor Chair in Education in the Graduate School of Education at Rutgers University, USA.

Fred A. Bonner II is Professor and the Samuel DeWitt Proctor Endowed Chair in Education at the Graduate School of Education at Rutgers University, the State University of New Jersey. Dr. Bonner's work has been featured both nationally and internationally and he has been the recipient of numerous awards.

Throughout his career, Dr. Bonner's work has consistently been centered on microcultural populations developing attitudes, motivations, and strategies to survive in macrocultural settings. Dr. Bonner's book *Academically Gifted African American Male College Students* highlights the experiences of postsecondary gifted African American male undergraduates in predominantly White and Historically Black college contexts. In the fall of 2011, he released *Diverse Millennial Students in College*. His most recent work, *Building Resilience: Models and Frameworks of Black Males' Success across the P-20 Pipeline*, will be released May 2014.

Among his many professional service-oriented activities, Dr. Bonner serves in different editorial capacities for various journals; he is the Vice President for Research for the American Association of Blacks in Higher Education (AABHE), and is a member of the North Carolina A&T School of Education Advisory Board.

As the Samuel Dewitt Proctor Chair in Education and in continuing with his professional work, Dr. Bonner's aim is to promote potential through campus, local, national, and global community partnerships.

J. Yasmine Butler, Ph.D. is Assistant Professor at Sam Houston State University in Huntsville, Texas, where she is primarily responsible for teaching cross-cultural, school counseling and practica courses. She heads the school counseling program in the Department of Educational Leadership & Counseling. Yasmine is licensed as a Professional Counselor and certified as a Professional School

Counselor. She received her Ph.D. in Counselor Education from the Ohio State University in 2010. Her research agenda focuses on curriculum, instruction, and technology. Additionally, she studies the integration of spirituality, culture, and health sciences. This research includes an interdisciplinary approach to studying the human experience of faith, beliefs, attitudes, and spirituality in the context of counseling and other health sciences.

Dorinda J. Carter Andrews is Associate Professor in the Department of Teacher Education at Michigan State University, where she teaches courses on racial identity development, urban education, critical multiculturalism, and critical race theory. She is also a Core Faculty member in MSU's African American and African Studies program and a Faculty Leader in the Urban Educators Cohort Program, a program designed to prepare MSU preservice students for teaching careers in urban contexts. Dr. Carter's research is broadly focused on race and educational equity. She studies issues of educational equity in suburban and urban schools, urban teacher preparation and identity development, and critical race praxis with K-12 educators. Dr. Carter also values civic engagement and community outreach and was awarded the 2014 Michigan State University Scholarship Community Partnership Award for her work with school districts to close academic achievement gaps.

Dr. Carter Andrews is a former industrial engineer, high school math teacher, and kindergarten teacher and has teaching experience in suburban, urban, charter, and independent schools in metropolitan Atlanta, Nashville, and Boston. As an educational consultant, she has partnered with urban and suburban school districts with varying student demographics to address student achievement inequities and build culturally inclusive environments where staff and students are focused on becoming more culturally responsive. She regularly conducts professional development for in-service educators on how to better address the academic and social needs of culturally diverse students in various educational contexts and engage in courageous conversations and action about the implications of race and bias in schools.

Dr. Carter Andrews is a recipient of the 2014 Early Career Contribution Award from the Committee on Scholars of Color in Education of the American Educational Research Association. She is also a 2013–2014 Phi Delta Kappa Emerging Leader and a recipient of the 2014 Alumni of Color Achievement Award from the Harvard Graduate School of Education Alumni of Color Conference. She is an editor and contributing author of *Contesting the Myth of a "Post Racial Era": The Continued Significance of Race in U. S. Education* (2013). Her work has been published in top-tier journals such as *Harvard Educational Review*, *Teachers College Record*, *Journal of Negro Education*, and *Anthropology & Education Quarterly*, among others.

Natasha N. Croom, Ph.D. is Assistant Professor in the Higher Education and Student Affairs programs in the School of Education at Iowa State University.

148

Her scholarship focuses on the experiences of black women across postsecondary contexts and the theoretical and practical applications of critical race feminism in higher education research and student affairs practice. Dr. Croom's research on the post-tenure advancement experiences of black female faculty garnered the 2011 American Association of Blacks in Higher Education Dissertation of the Year Award. Her work has been published in peer-reviewed journals such as *Negro Educational Review* and *Equity & Excellence in Education*.

Alonzo M. Flowers III, Ph.D. is Assistant Professor in the Department of Educational Leadership, Counseling, and Foundations at the University of New Orleans. Dr. Flowers specializes in educational issues including poverty and academic giftedness of African American males, STEM education, diversity, and college student transition and development. Dr. Flowers' research focuses on the academic experiences of academically gifted African American and Latino students in the STEM disciplines, particularly engineering, mathematics, and science. He has completed 35 peer-reviewed conference presentations since 2005. This includes several national presentations at the Association for the Study of Higher Education and Texas Association for the Gifted and Talented state conference. Recently, he was selected to be the keynote speaker at the first annual Texas African American Males in College Achievement & Success Symposium in Austin, Texas, where he discussed Giftedness at a Crossroads for African American Male College Students in STEM.

Mark Giles is Associate Professor and interdisciplinary educator-scholar in the Department of Educational Leadership and Policy Studies at the University of Texas at San Antonio. His research interests include 20th century African American history, critical race theory, the intersections of leadership and spirituality, and the social, cultural, and political contexts of education (K-20). He teaches across the program areas of African American Studies, Educational Leadership, Higher Education, and Social Foundations.

Katherine Helm is Professor of Psychology and Director of Graduate Programs in Psychology at Lewis University, where she happily teaches a wide range of graduate and undergraduate counseling and psychology courses. Dr. Helm is also a licensed psychologist. She regularly sees individual clients and couples and supervises a clinical training program for master's and doctoral practicum students. Dr. Helm's scholarly contributions and interests are in the areas of: individual and couples counseling, sexuality issues and education, training and supervision, multicultural issues in counseling, the treatment of trauma for sexual abuse, pedagogy of multicultural courses, and cultural sensitivity training.

Shih-Han Huang is a doctoral candidate and Research Assistant of Counselor Education in the Department of Education Psychology and Leadership at Texas

Tech University. She is originally from Taiwan and came to the United States to pursue her master, and doctoral degrees in 2007. She holds a bachelor of social work from Tung Hai University in Taiwan. Her research interests are social class, gender issues, multicultural counseling competence, and social justice. Shih-Han Huang anticipates graduating with her Ph.D. in Counselor Education in 2015.

Robin L. Hughes is Associate Professor in the Department of Educational Leadership and Policy Studies, Higher Education Student Affairs (HESA) at Indiana University Indianapolis, USA.

Anton Lewis is Assistant Professor of Accounting at Saint Xavier University, Chicago. For his dissertation research, Dr. Lewis utilized critical race theory to investigate the experience of Black accountants in the UK through qualitative methods. Future research goals include expanding research to develop critical models and conceptual frameworks of multicultural diversity of accountants in government bodies and accountancy organizations in the United States. Dr. Lewis is currently studying a research sample of professional Black accountants in the United States for a forthcoming pilot study. Dr. Lewis recently published a book in 2012, titled *A Critical Analysis of the Black Accounting Experience in the U.K.: Tales of Success and Failure in the British Professional Workplace.*

Jiaqi Li is Assistant Professor in the Department of Counseling, Educational Leadership, Educational and School Psychology in the College of Education at Wichita State University. He received his Ph.D. in Counselor Education and Supervision at Texas Tech University. His research focuses on multiculturalism, professional school counseling, Asian international students and immigrants, ethics, and Posttraumatic Stress Disorder (PTSD).

aretha faye marbley is Professor and Director of Community Counseling in Counselor Education at Texas Tech University. She is a critical social justice womanist activist, scholar storyteller, and clinical counselor educator. She has authored the book *Multicultural Counseling: Perspectives from Counselors as Clients of Color* and co-edited the recently released *Diverse Millennial Students in College: Implications for Faculty and Student Affairs.* She has been an invited participant on social, human, cultural, and social justice rights and issues for international organizations such as the United Nations, World Bank, Salzburg Global Seminars. She has received numerous communities and academic awards including the Texas Tech University President's Academic Award, Office of the President's Excellence in Diversity and Equity Faculty Award, and twice the Texas Tech Outstanding Researcher Award. She is also the recipient of two national awards, one focusing on research and the other on human rights. Marbley has also received the Anti-Oppression on Social Justice Award and the Texas Counselors for Social Justice Award.

150

Ariel W. Moore is Associate Professor of Postsecondary Administration at a large, public research institution in the Southwestern United States. Moore has published several books and numerous peer reviewed journal articles focused on student success for historically underrepresented and underserved students. In particular, his research focuses on student retention and achievement among men of color in postsecondary education. Dr. Moore is an editor of an academic journal as well as teaching courses on quantitative research methods and program evaluation.

James L. Moore III, Ph.D., LPCC-S, PSC is Associate Provost in the Office of Diversity and Inclusion, where he also serves as the inaugural director of the Todd Anthony Bell National Resource Center on the African American Male at the Ohio State University. Additionally, Dr. Moore is the EHE Distinguished Professor of Urban Education in the College of Education and Human Ecology. He has a national- and international-recognized research agenda that focuses on school counseling, gifted education, urban education, higher education, multicultural education/counseling, and STEM education. He recently co-edited two books with Dr. Chance W. Lewis of the University of North Carolina at Charlotte, titled *African American Students in Urban Schools: Critical Issues and Solutions for Achievement* and *African American Male Students in PreK-12 Schools: Informing Research, Policy, and Practice*. Further, Dr. Moore has published over 100 publications, obtained over $8 million in grants, contracts, gifts, and given over 200 scholarly presentations and lectures throughout the United States and other parts of the world.

Lori D. Patton, Ph.D. is Associate Professor in the Higher Education and Student Affairs program at the Indiana University School of Education. She has presented over 100 research papers, workshops, symposia and keynote addresses and has been recognized nationally for research examining issues of identity, equity, and racial injustice affecting diverse populations in postsecondary institutions. Her scholarship on black culture centers, critical race theory, LGBT students of color, and African American women has been published in top peer-reviewed journals including the *Journal of College Student Development*, *Journal of Higher Education*, and *Journal of Negro Education*, as well as numerous books. Dr. Patton was awarded the 2010 ASHE Promising Scholar/Early Career Award and the 2008 Mildred E. Garcia Award for Exemplary Scholarship. She is affiliated with and highly involved in numerous professional associations. She earned her Ph.D. in Higher Education (Indiana University), M.A. in College Student Personnel (Bowling Green State University), and B.S. in Speech Communication (Southern Illinois University at Edwardsville).

Petra A. Robinson is Assistant Professor in the School of Human Resource Education and Workforce Development at Louisiana State University, USA.

151

Leon Rouson is Associate Professor in the Department of Early Childhood, Elementary and Special Education, and Principal Investigator/Executive Director of the Teacher PREP Student Support Services Project at Norfolk State University. He completed both his bachelor's and master's degrees from North Carolina Central University in Durham, NC, and his Ph.D. from Old Dominion University in Norfolk, VA. He has done further studies and research at East Carolina University in Greenville, NC and the University of North Carolina at Chapel-Hill.

Marjorie C. Shavers, Ph.D., LPCC-S, PSC is Assistant Professor at Heidelberg University in the counseling program. She has a Ph.D. in Counselor Education from the Ohio State University and is currently a licensed professional clinical counselor and licensed as a professional school counselor. Dr. Shavers has had many academic, clinical, and personal experiences that have contributed to her research interests. Her research agenda is divided into two distinct, yet interrelated, strands: (a) studying how educational professionals and administrators can influence the experiences and overall well-being of students of color, particularly African American women; and (b) examining ways that individuals, in general, and minority students in particular use technology to explore and manage identity and foster communication and relationships. Consequently, Dr. Shavers' career is dedicated to improving the experiences of students and using her work as a counselor to address social and emotional needs.

Buffy Smith is Associate Professor in the Department of Sociology and Criminal Justice at the University of St. Thomas. She earned her B.A. in Sociology at Marquette University and an M.S. and Ph.D. in Sociology at the University of Wisconsin-Madison. Dr. Smith's primary research interests include examining racial and class disparities within the higher education system. She also writes on policy issues dealing with mentoring, access, retention, equity, and diversity in higher education. Dr. Smith's publications have been featured in research and practice-oriented journals such as *African-American Research Perspectives* and *Equity & Excellence in Education*. In addition, she is the author of the book *Mentoring At-Risk Students through the Hidden Curriculum of Higher Education* (2013).

Dafina-Lazarus Stewart, Ph.D. has been Associate Professor in the Department of Higher Education and Student Affairs at Bowling Green State University since 2005. Dr. Stewart focuses her research on issues of diversity and social justice, particularly through the lenses of race and ethnicity, sexuality and gender, and religion and faith as they are related to identity, student outcomes, and institutional transformation informed by an intersectional perspective. Dr. Stewart publishes widely in higher education journals and regularly presents at conferences and workshops across the country. She has published an edited volume on multicultural affairs, *Multicultural*

Student Services on Campus: Building Bridges, Re-visioning Community (2011) and is currently working to complete an oral history of the experiences of Black collegians at private, elite, liberal arts colleges in the Great Lakes region between 1945 and 1965.

Colette M. Taylor earned her B.S. in Psychology, MEd in Counselor Education and EdD. in Educational Leadership from the University of Florida. She is a co-editor of *African Americans and Community Engagement in Higher Education* (2009). Currently, she serves as an associate professor of higher education at Texas Tech University. She spent 14 years as a student affairs professional, working in residence life, student activities, and a dean of students office before becoming a faculty member in 2008. Prior to her faculty appointment, Dr. Taylor served two years at Middle Tennessee State University as Assistant Vice President/Associate Dean of Students. She has previously held positions at University of Florida, Nova Southeastern University, and Wake Forest University.

Saundra M. Tomlinson-Clarke is Associate Professor and licensed psychologist. She teaches in the Programs in School Counseling and Counseling Psychology in the Department of Educational Psychology at Rutgers Graduate School of Education. Prior to joining the faculty at Rutgers, the State University of New Jersey, she was employed as a staff psychologist and provided counseling and support services to students on university campuses. Dr. Tomlinson-Clarke's research focuses training models that prepare counselors, psychologists, and teachers to more effectively serve culturally diverse learners. Focused on the psychosocial adjustment and achievement, her work applies to learners in middle school, high school, and college. She has received several grants exploring the integration of the arts and STEM with an emphasis on pedagogical practices that increase teacher effectiveness, and learner engagement. Her work extends to international communities, and transformative learning experiences that promote social change and social justice advocacy.

Frank Tuitt is Associate Professor of Higher Education and Associate Provost for Inclusive Excellence at the University of Denver, USA.

Index

academic comfort 55–6
academic culture shock 62
academic haterism 70–1, 75
accents 33–4, 33–5
advocacy 26
affirmative action viii, 26–7
African American history, benefits of
    studying 16
Africana Womanism 56, 58, 59, 64
Afro-American Studies 16, 18
Aguirre Jr., A. 41
Alabama 29
alienation 41, 55, 116, 121, 139
Allen, D. 123
allyship 99
Ambrose, S. 107
And We Are Not Saved (Bell) 16
Angry Black Woman (ABW) stereotype
    36, 37
Antonio, A. L. 109
anxiety 62
authenticity 86, 90, 91, 98, 99, 121

Baez, B. 26
Banda, Rosie M. 105, 107, 108–9,
    110, 112
Banning, H. 134
Barber, E. 109
barriers, breaking 59
battles, choosing 64
Beaumont, Texas 24
beauty, standards of 71–3, 75–6, 89

Bell, Derrick 2, 16, 29
belongingness 14, 24
Bieber, J. P. 109
Black Britishness 33–4
Black femininity 36
Black feminist respectability 90–1
Black feminist thought (BFT) 6, 68–9, 80,
    80–1, 90, 97
Black Male Fetish 73–4, 76
Black masculinity 89
Black on stage 37, 38, 39
Black queer women 118, 121; authenticity
    90, 91, 98, 99; coming out 90–2;
    experience of 89–98; fetishizing 92–3;
    fitting in 90–1; gender presentation
    92; graduate school experience 116–8;
    hyper-visibility 96; invisibility 89,
    96–7, 119; outsider[s]-within 94–6;
    recommendations 99; representation
    of 89–99; stereotypes 93–5; support
    networks 99
Black Student Association 138
Black students, advocates 26
black tax 38
Blackburn, R. 109
Blackness 33–5, 37, 60–2, 89, 97
Bo Derek Effect, the 71–3, 75–6
Bonner, F. A. II. 126, 128, 129–30,
    131–2, 133
Boyer, Earnest 59, 63
Brown v. Board of Education, Topeka Kansas 2,
    19–20

Business Administration 18
Butler, J. 90

California 23, 30–1
candid conversations 106–9
Carbado, D. 37, 38
career-related stressors 105
challenges 33
children's literature 18
Chinese students 62
Cincinnati, University of 15, 17–9
citations 75
Clance, P. R. 117
classroom presentation 37
code switching 131–2
Cole, S. 109
Coleman, James 117
collaboration 75, 106
Collins, P. 72, 76–7, 80, 85, 95, 97, 98
colorblindness 2, 4, 15, 34
colorism 70
commitment 21
committee membership 39, 41, 42, 45,
    46, 47, 111, 120, 130
competence 33, 64, 126–7
competition 70–1
condescension 81–2
conflict 1–2
contracts 26
control 31
coping mechanisms 18–9, 31
counseling 142, 143
counter-narratives ix, 3–4, 57, 112
credibility 140
Crenshaw, K. W. 16–7, 72, 76–7
critical consciousness lens 21
critical dialogue exchanges 105, 106–9
critical feminist theory 5, 55, 57–8,
    58, 63
critical legal scholarship 69
critical mentoring relationships 6–7
critical race feminism (CRF) 6, 57, 68,
    69–70, 76–7
critical race theory (CRT) vii, viii–ix, 55,
    56, 58, 69, 76, 90, 133, 137, 140;
    application 4–7; counter-narratives ix,
    3–4; definition 17; methodology 3,

4–7; and systemic racism 15–7; tenets
2, 17
critical relationships: early influences
    137–8, 143; establishing 141–2;
    recommendations 142–3; as a student
    138–41; with students 137–43;
    women 141
critical theory 56, 63
cultural climates 13, 14, 133–4
cultural norms 96
cultural survival 16
cultural taxation 5, 41–9, 125;
    description 42–3; just say no 44–5,
    48–9; mutually beneficial mentoring
    46–7, 49; and quick decisions 47, 49;
    and scholarship agenda 45–6, 48–9;
    service expectations 42, 43–4, 44;
    strategies to address 44–8; unspoken
    expectations 47–8; unwritten rules
    49; women 43
cultural connections 81–2
culture 34
curriculum development viii–ix

Davidson, W. 46
de Saxe, J. 57
Delgado, R. 16–7
denigration 82
departmental initiatives 7
Derek, Bo 71
desegregation 20
dialogue, diversity in 109
differential racialization 69, 71
Diggs, G. 131, 134
Dillard, C. B. 68–9, 76–7
discipline viii
dissertation committees 130
Diverse Issues 73
diversity 15, 20, 31, 48, 84, 85; and
    the commodification of race 43; in
    dialogue 109
diversity committees 29–30, 41, 42,
    111
domination 75, 95
double oppression 80–1
double-consciousness 132
DuBois, W.E.B. 132

editorial feedback 55
educational attainment 20
emotional costs 38
employment, longevity of 105
empowerment 63, 142
endarkened feminist epistemologies 68, 68–9, 75, 76–7
ethic of critique, the 27
ethics 27
evaluations 27–8
exclusion 5, 24, 57, 129–31, 139
experiential knowledge 2
expertise 95–6
exploitation 13

Faces at the Bottom of the Well (Bell) 16
faculty dining 28
faculty expertise 95–6
faculty life, transition into 25
faculty ranks 20
failure, fear of 21
fairness 126
Felder, P. 141
feminist legal theory 69
feminist theory 57, 58
first-person voice viii
fitting in vii, 1–2, 37–8, 90–1, 110–1
focus 21

gender 6
gender construction 81
gender expression 96
gender inequities 57
gender insubordination 96
gender microaggressions 29, 31, 79–87
gender privilege 73–4, 76
gendered racial battle fatigue 79–80, 81, 83
gendered racism 79
Geuss, R. 56
good intentions 20
graduate school experience 116–8
group advantage 2
group disadvantage 2
Guinier, L. 69
Gulati, M. 37, 38

Hagedorn, L. S. 105, 111
hidden curriculum, the 6, 85, 117, 119, 121
hierarchy viii
higher education, development of 56
hiring policies 20, 25, 26–7
historical legacies 5, 24
Historically Black College and University (HBCU) 60–2, 139
history, presentation of ix
Hollins, E. 129
homosexuality 116, 118, 121; authenticity 90–2, 91, 98, 99; coming out 90–2; experience of 89–98; fitting in 90–1; gender presentation 92; hyper-visibility 96; invisibility 96–7; outsider[s]-within 94–6; recommendations 99; representation of 89–99; stereotypes 93–5; support networks 99
hooks, b. 77, 97, 127
hope 124
Howard-Hamilton, Mary 130–1
Hudson-Weems, C. 58, 64
Hughes, Robin 130
Hurtado, A. 72
Huston, T. 107
hyper-visibility 96

identity vii, 98; construction 70; multiple 72, 75, 79, 95, 131–3; personal 140–1; professional 7; scholarly 70, 85–6; shared 140; working 37–8, 38, 39
identity performance 92, 97
Imes, S. 117
impact 59
imposter syndrome 117
inappropriate behavior, mentors 81–2
inclusion 131, 134
inclusive exclusion 84–6
insider status 39
institutional climate vii, 5, 13–21, 41, 83, 143; chilly 14, 133–4; focus 19; good intentions 20; historical background 13–4; lack of change 20; literature 14; recommendations 20–1; and

systemic racism 15–7; undergraduate experience 17–9; unintentional coldness 19; unwelcoming environment 19
institutional racism 56
institutional settings vii, 111
institutional support 31
integration 107
intellectual mode 64
interdisciplinary approaches 5–6
Interest Convergence 29
interpersonal racial oppression 142
intersectional approaches 5–6
intersectionality 69
intersectionality theory 70, 72, 75, 76, 95
intimidating 35–6, 37
intraracial discrimination 70
invisibility 89, 96–7, 119
isolation 6, 24, 62, 106–8

Jennings, Michael 130
Jim Crow era 61
job satisfaction 105
job searches 118
Johnson, T. 74
jokes 28
Josselson, Ruthellen 106
journaling 31

Kaba, A. J. 74
Kamau, N. M. 133
knowable, being 39
knowledge production 69
knowledgeable 36, 36–7
Kramarae, C. 57

Laden, B. V. 111
Ladson-Billings, G. ix, 68, 76
Laszloffy, T. 44
Lawrence, C. R., III 16–7
leadership 27, 29
legitimation struggles 81–3
level playing field, illusion of 4
liberation theology 28
likeability 86
lived experiences viii, ix, 1, 3–4, 57, 106
Logginton, California 23–4

Lorde, A. 90
Louque, A. C. 128
loyalty 26

macro invalidations 5
Mammy figure 94–5
marginality 5, 24, 95, 97
marginalization 56, 63, 70, 70–1, 80, 133–4, 135
Martin, Trayvon 37
Matsuda, M. J. 16–7
meaning making 5–6, 69
men, gender privilege 73–4, 76
mentors and mentoring 21, 39, 45, 111; critical relationships 138–9, 141; and cultural taxation 125; dialogue 125; direction 127; and exclusion 129–31; expectations 119; experience of 126–34; faculty relationships 128–9; feedback 119; graduate school experience 116–8; identifying 86; importance of 64, 111, 119–20, 123–35; inappropriate behavior 81–2; informal 119–20; and institutional climate 133–4; job searches 118; junior faculty member experience 118–20; and multiple identities 131–3; mutually beneficial 46–7, 49; networks 120; real talk 127; recommendations 120–1, 134–5; relationships 115–21; respect 119; role 123, 135; self-worth support 126–7; social capital 117–8, 121; urgency 124–5
meritocracy ix, 2, 4
microaggressions 133; academic culture shock 62; experience of 58–62; Historically Black College and/nlUniversity (HBCU) 60–2; negotiating 55–64; publication 58–60; theoretical perpectives 56–8; see also gender microaggressions; race-gendered microaggressions; racial microaggressions
micro-assaults 24, 28
micro-insults 24, 28
micro-invalidations 24–5, 27, 30

minority status 41
model minority myth 74, 76
Moya, P. M. L. 98
multicultural competence 140–1
multiculturalism 61
multiple identities 72, 75, 79, 95, 131–3
multiple marginality vii, 1
multiple oppressions vii, 1
mutually beneficial mentoring 49
Myers, S. L., Jr. vii, 128, 131

Nash, R. J. 3
Naylor, G. 89
NCATE standards 29
negation 30
networks, informal 138, 142
Norman, M. 107

Obama, Barack 28, 73
Obama, Michelle 133
objectivity 2, 4
occupational stress 43
opportunity 57
oppositional scholarship 58
oppression 5, 13, 16, 57, 75, 95, 121, 142
otherness 1, 7
outreach 45–6
outsider[s]-within 94–6, 98
outsider-insiders 33–5
over sensitivity, perceived 29
over-commitment 41–9; cultural taxation
    42–3; just say no 44–5, 48–9;
    mutually beneficial mentoring 46–7,
    49; and quick decisions 47, 49; and
    scholarship agenda 45–6, 49; service
    expectations 43–4, 44; strategies to
    address 44–8; unspoken expectations
    47–8; unwritten rules 49

Padilla, A. M. 42
passionate 35–6
passive aggressiveness 33
patriarchy 57
Patton, L. 74, 130
Patton, S. 74
peer support 138, 139–40
perceptual environment, the 134

persistence 21
personal identity 140–1
Personal Identity, Dimensions of 137
Phelan, P. 90
Pittman, C. T. 142
positioning, women 72–3
post-racial assumptions 15
power relations 31, 57, 69
prejudice 29–30
predominantly White institutions (PWIs)
    1, 61, 106, 133; advancements 19;
    Black female faculty 79–87; critical
    relationships 138–41; cultural taxation
    41–9; focus 19; good intentions
    20; institutional climate 5, 13–21;
    lack of change 20; service expectations
    42, 43–4, 44; unwelcoming
    environment 19
pride 24
prior awareness 31
Proctor, Samuel DeWitt 135
productivity 46
professional credibility 140
professional development 46
professional identity, development of 7
promotion policies 20
psychological costs 38
psychological well-being 31, 127
psychologically damaging discourse
    29–30
publication 31, 55, 58–60, 71, 110

queer people of color (QPOC) 89–99

race: commodification of 43; construction
    81; social construction of 69
race neutrality 2, 5
race-based stress 129
race-gendered microaggressions 79–87;
    experience of 81–6; inclusive
    exclusion 84–6; legitimation struggles
    81–3; recommendations 86–7
race-related service 43
racial attacks 30
racial battle fatigue 79–80, 81, 83, 142
racial gap 41
racial justice-oriented legislation 20

racial microaggressions 4–5, 23–31, 93, 142; cumulative effects 15; definition 24, 80; experience of 25–30; meanings 31; micro-assaults 24, 28; micro-insults 24, 28; micro-invalidations 24–5, 27, 30; types 24–5
racial oppression, elimination of 2, 7
racial solidarity 93
racialized expectations 142
racialized isolation 6
racialized landscapes 24
racialized presence 37
racialized society 140
racially-based communication: *see* micro-insults
racism 2, 3, 13; daily encounters with 4–5; institutional 56; pervasive 14; systemic 15–7, 37; threats in the air 4–5; undergraduate experience 18–9
racist sexism 79, 81–2
Reagan, Ronald 60
real talk 127
recognition, lack of 83
reflection 75, 105–12, 109; critical 143; dialogues 106–9; fitting in 110–1; publication 110
relationship building 36–7
relocation, difficulties of 107–8
representation 130; lack of 42–3
respect, lack of 55, 139
rewards 6
Rockquemore, K. A. 44
role-models 62, 141
rules of engagement 124

safe space 134
Sapphire stereotype 36, 37
scholarly identity 70, 85–6
scholarly manner 64
Scholarly Personal Narrative (SPN) viii, 3–4
scholarly productivity 42
segregation 61
self-definition 58, 62, 63, 69, 89, 98, 99
self-knowledge 39
self-preservation 7
self-reflection 20, 105–12; critical 143; dialogues 106–9; and diversity

in dialogue 109; fitting in 110–1; publication 110
self-worth 126–7
senior-level leadership 20
service expectations 42, 43–4, 44; hidden 5; just say no 44–5, 48–9; pressure 47; and quick decisions 47, 49; and scholarship agenda 45–6, 48–9; unwritten rules 47–8, 49; using 45–6
sexism 14, 81–2
sexual discrimination 29
sexuality 89–99, 116, 118, 121
shared identity 140
sister circles 86
skepticism. 2
skin color 70–1, 75
slavery 13, 16
Smith, E. 46
Smith, W. A. 128
social acclimation 108–9
social capital 117–8, 121
social events 39, 115
social justice 19, 59, 109, 141
social networking 5, 33–9; recommendations 39; sister circles 86; and support 36–7; working identity 37–8
social support 112
social transformation 7
socialization 70, 137, 138
Sojourner, Truth vii
Solórzano, D. 3
standardized testing ix
standards 1
Stanley, C. A. vii, 1, 80, 128, 130–1
status 126
Strange, C. 134
strength 87; rediscovering 63–4
stress 62, 105, 129
structural inequalities 5
student concerns, and affirmative action 26–7
student diversity 29
student stereotypes 33–4
students: closed-minded 33–4; commitment 138; development promotion 143; empowerment 142; expectations 142; othermothering

141; relationships with 137–43; support 46
subjectification 97
subordination viii
Sue, D. W. 24–5, 73, 142
Sue, S. 140
support networks 21, 45, 86, 99, 106–7, 109, 112, 120, 138
systemic racism 15–7, 37

tenacity 87
Tennessee 25
tenure policies 20, 26, 44, 70, 124, 127
Thompson, G. L. 128
Thurman, Wallace 67–8, 70
Tillman, L. 82, 85
Tinto, V. 107
togetherness 139
token voice 42
Torres, G. 69
trailing spouse agreements 25–6
transparency 111
Tuitt, F. 112
Turner, C. S. V. vii, 128, 131
two-society track 19–20
typecasting 110

UMOJA 138
university awards 82–3
unspoken expectations 47–8
unwritten rules 47–8, 49, 117

voice viii, 42, 59

Wenzel, S. 109
White privilege 56

White spaces 14–5
White supremacy 56, 81
White women 72, 81, 84–5, 118–9
wholeness 62
Wilder, C. 13
Wittig, M. 96
women 5–6; academic comfort 55–6; and academic haterism 70–1, 75; critical relationships 141; cultural taxation 43; doctorates 137; experiences 79–87; and gender privilege 73–4, 76; gendered racial battle fatigue 79–80; inclusive exclusion 81–3; legitimation struggles 81–3; Mammy figure 94–5; marginalization 56; microaggressions 55–64; model minority myth 74, 76; outsider status 89; perspectives 67–77; positioning 72–3; racial microaggressions 93; self-definition 58, 63, 69, 89; self-naming 58, 63; social networks 36–7; standards of beauty 71–3, 75–6, 89; status 73, 89; stereotypes 36, 37, 89, 93–5; success 74; White 72, 81, 84–5, 118–9; working identity 37–8
Wood, J. T. 57
Words that Wound (Matsuda et al) 16–7
working identity 37–8, 39
work–life balance 108
Wright, Reverend Jeremiah 28

Yosso, T. 3
Young, I. M. 90

Zane, N. 140
Zimmerman, George 73

Printed by PGSTL